The System

*The Proven 3-Step Formula
Anyone Can Learn to Get More Leads,
Book More Appointments, and Make More Sales*

Eric Lofholm

Foreword by Dr. Donald Moine

ERIC LOFHOLM INTERNATIONAL

Foreword by Dr. Donald Moine
Editorial direction by Roy Rasmussen
Interior design and layout by Marian Hartsough
Cover design by Diego Rodriguez based on a design by Roy Rasmussen

Disclaimer: This book is intended to provide information only, and should not be construed as professional sales or business advice. No income claims are stated or implied. How you put this information to use is up to you.

ISBN-10: 0-9898942-0-7
ISBN-13: 978-0-9898942-0-3

Printed in the United States of America

Eric Lofholm
Eric Lofholm International
5701 Lonetree Blvd. Suite 121
Rocklin, CA 95765 United States
(916) 626-6820

Contents

PART III: Action   143

Part IV: Bonus Material   153

Dedication

To the millions of people out there whose income is directly tied to their ability to persuade others.

Acknowledgments

I would like to acknowledge and thank all those who have influenced my understanding of sales and persuasion, including especially my mentors Dante Perano, Dr. Donald Moine, Tony Martinez, and Jay Abraham; as well as Tony Robbins, Michael Gerber, and Ted Thomas.

Most of all I would like to thank my mother and father; and my children Brandon and Sarah, whose love and support has inspired this book.

Foreword by Dr. Donald Moine

It gives me great pleasure to write this foreword for Eric Lofholm's book.

When we write a book, we stand on the shoulders of those who came before us. When I wrote my first book with John Herd, *Modern Persuasion Strategies*, John Herd and I stood on the shoulders of the brilliant behavioral scientists Richard Bandler and John Grinder, who had created NLP. John Herd and I wrote a book that was, to the best of my knowledge, the first book a major publisher had ever published on Neuro-Linguistic Programming (NLP) applied to master salesmanship.

When I wrote my second book, *Unlimited Selling Power*, with Dr. Ken Lloyd, Ken and I stood on the shoulders of Dr. Milton Erickson, the father of indirect or conversational hypnosis. *Unlimited Selling Power* was the first book ever on how sales superstars use powerful forms of indirect and conversational hypnosis, such as hypnotic stories and metaphors, to outsell other salespeople.

In asking me to write this foreword, Eric Lofholm said that he learned a great deal about master salesmanship from my work and our work together. I, in turn, have learned much from Eric during the 20+ years I have known him.

How I met Eric and the story of his rise to prominence as a sales trainer is a fascinating story in and of itself.

I first met Eric Lofholm when I was working as a coach to Tony Martinez and Dante Perano in the early 1990s. At the time, Dante was one of the top real estate investors and real estate educators in America. Tony Martinez was one of his employees and a rising star in the real estate education industry. Dante had a very popular television show on real estate investing and he was leading seminars all over the United States.

At that time, Eric Lofholm was an employee of Dante's company and it was Eric's job to help set up hotel conference rooms and ball rooms for big speaking events. Eric arranged the tables, set out educational material, handled book sales at the back of the room, packed and unpacked boxes of books and took care of dozens of other details that are involved in setting up seminars for hundreds of attendees.

Another way of describing Eric's job is to say that Eric was a "go-fer" whose job it was to go out and do anything and everything required to make sure the seminar rooms were set up properly and that seminar sales were handled properly.

While it was an important job, it didn't carry much status. In my work as a coach to sales superstars, I meet a lot of these "back of the room" people. I always treat them with courtesy but in most cases, I don't get to know most of them very well.

Eric Lofholm Rises from Failure to Success as a Sales Professional

There was something about Eric that made him stand out from all of the other back-of-the-room workers. He did his job exceptionally well and seemed to be able to effortlessly juggle dozens of responsibilities simultaneously in the high-stress environment of seminar selling. Eric and I had a few conversations and I found him to be a bright young man but I really knew virtually nothing about his goals beyond doing his job well.

At the time, I was concentrating all of my energies on working with Dante Perano, Tony Martinez and my other clients around the country. As I continued to work with Dante and Tony, sales for Dante's real estate education company began to soar and Dante's company started making more than $10 million a year in business. Tony Martinez went from being a low-income novice speaker to earning more than $100,000 a year (which was a lot of money back in the early 1990s for a man in his early 20s). Over the next couple of years as I did more work with Tony, he went on to earn several hundred thousand dollars per year.

While a lot of the back-of-the room employees didn't pay much attention to the speakers when they were making their presentations on stage, I noticed that Eric Lofholm was listening intently and was taking detailed notes on almost everything they said. I had no idea what Eric's motivation was. As a back-of-the-room employee, he obviously didn't have enough money to become a real estate investor.

Eric then got a job with Dante Perano doing sales. Unfortunately, Eric was a failure and was put on probation due to his low sales numbers. *His job was at risk.*

Then one day I was surprised when Eric told me he wanted to hire me to be his sales coach and to help him develop the powerful persuasion skills he saw Dante Perano and Tony Martinez using. I didn't see how Eric could possibly afford to hire me as his coach. Back in the early 1990s my rate was $250 an hour.

Where there is a will, there is a way. Somehow Eric was able to save up enough money to hire me to coach him. Our first session together was just for a couple of hours. Yet Eric was such a good student of the persuasion strategies I taught that his sales started to increase rapidly. He then had enough money to hire me for a few more hours the next week and a few more hours each week in the weeks after that.

Later that year, Eric became the #1 sales producer in Dante Perano's company.

I thought Eric would be satisfied with his newfound sales success. But he was already setting his sights even higher. The next year (when Eric was still in his early 20s), Eric decided to set up his own telemarketing company and to hire salespeople to work for him. He wanted to sell seminar seats for Dante Perano and other top seminar speakers around the country with the goal of filling their conference rooms to *maximum* capacity.

As you may know, telemarketing is a *very* challenging business. Telemarketing burns out salespeople at a more rapid pace than perhaps any other type of sales work. When you make phone calls hour after hour, day after day, you have to deal with an incredible amount of abuse and rejection.

Some people call you names or cuss you out. Speaking to a salesperson on the phone, some people believe they have a right to dish out profanities and to call you names. It takes a very strong person to make 100 sales calls or more per day and to attempt to do sales presentations to people who often weren't expecting your call. As one top telephone salesperson I was coaching told me, "You need to have a hide like a rhino to do this work!"

How Eric Lofholm Learned Master Salesmanship

I am sharing these details about Eric's life and his career with you for a very important reason. When someone tells you that he or she is an expert in selling, you want to know the *basis* for that claim. **How** *did they learn so much about selling?*

In my case, I worked my way through ten years of college as a salesman, from a first semester freshman all the way through my Ph.D. program. I sold large 10,000 gallon underground gasoline storage tanks, I then sold electronics parts for JVC (I did a lot of this work through telemarketing various companies), I sold books and tapes for tapes for the famous sales trainer Tom Hopkins and then I sold seminars for top NLP experts around the country.

As a professional sales trainer for the past 30 years, I have sold my programs to Fortune 500 companies and to mid-sized and smaller companies. Sales training is a highly competitive business with several hundred self-appointed sales experts all competing with one another.

While I've learned a lot from all of the selling I've done, I've learned even more from working one-on-one as the coach to a large number of sales superstars in a wide variety of industries and professions over the past three decades. Many of my clients make a million dollars or more per year from selling. The sales strategies they have developed to achieve this level of sales stardom are truly amazing. I've been collecting, analyzing and teaching these powerful sales and persuasion strategies for 30 years.

While I have a lot of experience in direct selling, it pales in comparison to Eric Lofholm's in-the-trenches experience. While running his telemarketing company, Eric personally made more than 200 phone calls per day. Despite the rejection and hostility that all telemarketing salespeople encounter on a daily basis, Eric's hard work enabled him to set sales records.

In my career, I've only met a few other sales superstars who had the discipline and stamina to call more than 200 prospects per day for weeks and months on end, keeping detailed records on each person and diligently following up to get repeat sales. Just imagine how much your sales could increase if you made 200 phone calls per day!

When you encounter so many different kinds of people on the phone every day, you quickly develop an in-depth understanding of human psychology. To become a superstar in telephone sales, you must learn how to deal with *dozens* of different personality types of human beings. From making several hundred thousand phone calls over his career, Eric has acquired this in-depth knowledge.

Eric's ambitions soon extended beyond the world of telemarketing. He went to work for a variety of companies and usually rose to become one of their top salespeople and in some cases became the very top salesperson in the organization. Eric then got hired by Tony Robbins to help Tony fill seminar rooms around the country.

When people attend a Tony Robbins seminar with 500 or more people in attendance, they might think that the room automatically fills itself since Tony is so famous. That is not how these seminars get filled. Even famous speakers need a lot of help to fill seminar rooms.

When Tony Robbins hired Eric Lofholm, Tony already had a large sales crew to help him promote his seminars and sell seminar seats. Eric was just one of several dozen highly motivated salespeople working for Tony Robbins.

As you probably know, Tony Robbins does seminars all over the country. Before he travels to a city, he will send out a sales crew to work on filling the seminar in that city. The salespeople will fly into the city, book hotel rooms and then call every decent-sized business in town so that they can to get appointments to go out and do a free 30-minute sales training and sales presentation.

Tony's salespeople will go to auto dealerships, to real estate offices, to banks, to any business that has several salespeople and is open to letting someone come in and do a free 30-minute presentation. The presentation gives attendees a taste of what they are going to learn if they attend Tony Robbins' up-coming seminar.

At the end of the presentation, it is the job of the salesperson to try to sell tickets to the local Tony Robbins seminar. This is not as easy as you might think because some people say that they just saw Tony when he came to town last year, or they say that they already have Tony's CD's or DVD's and they know his message, or they say they read his book and know the content, or they say that they are too busy to go to the seminar or they have another objection or stall.

It is the job of Tony's salespeople to deal with all of these objections and stalls and to try to sell as many tickets as possible as quickly as possible. Once they finish that 30-minute presentation and sell some tickets, they have to drive off to another part of town to do another 30-minute presentation, then another one somewhere else and so on. Day after day, week after week they travel from city to city doing all these sales presentations. It is exhausting work, living on the road out of suitcases and working long days calling on a wide variety of businesses.

Eric reconnected with me again after he had been hired to be a seminar salesman for Tony Robbins. Eric told me he wanted to hire me to coach him to reach the highly competitive field of seminar selling. I had been working with famous seminar speakers and coaching their sales teams since the mid-1980s. While this demanding new sales profession challenged Eric, he worked hard to develop all of the sales skills essential for success in this highly specialized field. Within a couple of years, Eric was Tony Robbins #1 sales professional in his seminar promotion business.

To keep this as brief as possible, I've left out a number of Eric Lofholm's other notable sales achievements. But as you've learned, Eric as spent tens of thousands of hours *in the trenches* working as a sales professional and he has distinguished himself as one of the "best of the best" sales professionals in many different sales environments.

After watching me conduct a number of sales training seminars over the years and after watching Tony Robbins conduct many of his seminars, Eric decided to become a professional sales trainer himself in the early 2000's. In the succeeding years, Eric has risen to prominence as one of the top sales trainers in America today and in this book, he shares some of his timeless sales wisdom with you.

What Distinguishes Eric Lofholm's Sales Training

One of the key distinguishing traits of Eric Lofholm's sales training is that it is *extremely practical.* In this book, you won't encounter any theory or generalizations about selling. Eric presents a powerful *proven* formula for sales success.

Eric's training is also *easy to follow and master.* He presents his sales system in a simple but powerful series of steps. One of my criticisms of some sales trainers is that they have too many systems with too many steps that end up unnecessarily complicating the sales process and confusing the salespeople who try to use it.

For example, some sales trainers have 8 Steps to Prospecting. I've seen others teach 12 Steps to Doing the First Sales Call with a Prospect, 9 Steps in Discovering a Buyer's Motives, and 12 Steps to Closing. Other sales trainers teach 10 Steps in Pre-Qualifying a Prospect, 15 Questions You Need to Ask a Customer, 8 Steps to Set Up the Next Meeting, 9 Steps to Get Referrals, and various other multi-step sales systems.

It sometimes seems that the number of sales steps a sales trainer can create to teach salesmanship is limited only by the human imagination. In most cases, these overly-complex sales systems are almost impossible to remember and impractical to use in real life.

I've never met a top salesperson who followed such complex sales formulas.

The steps Eric presents like a breath of fresh air. They are simple to follow, powerful, practical and most importantly, *they get results!* Eric's students all over the country are powerful proof of this. If you visit Eric Lofholm's website, you'll sell many testimonials from his students in a wide variety of industries.

I'd also like to encourage you to visit Eric Lofholm's website to take in some of his powerful **free** online sales training. Eric does free webinars several times a month on topics that are of the greatest interest to sales professionals. People from all over the world attend Eric's webinars.

I estimate that I have been able to reach about 100,000 people through my books, articles and the seminars I have conducted around the United States, Canada, the Far East, Australia and Europe. Some of my books on master salesmanship have been translated into more than a dozen foreign languages and are sold around the world. Yet I have only been able to reach a fraction of the several hundred thousand people Eric Lofholm has reached through his sales training.

About twelve years ago, I decided to reduce my travel schedule and to cut back on the number of public seminars I offer so that I could concentrate on my coaching and consulting work with sales superstars. Some of the sales superstars I have worked with in the past few years have actually earned more than $10 million in *one* year from selling. I am not saying that they sold more than $10 million in products or services. I am saying that their commissions or gross income was more than $10 million in one year.

It is amazing how much money a sales champion can make today!

At least two of my clients have made more than $20 million a year from selling. And I have had more than two dozen clients who have earned more than $1 million a year. By the way, most of these ultra high-income clients are either in financial services, financial planning, insurance sales, annuity sales or seminar selling areas such as selling real estate investment strategies.

I don't judge people by how much money they make. I value my clients who earn $100,000 a year just as much as I value my clients who make many times that amount. I'm sharing these income numbers with you in the hopes that it may open your mind and inspire you to reach just a little higher in your own sales career.

Eric Lofholm has also worked with some of these ultra high-income sales superstars.

Through his use of webinars, Eric has been able to reach far more people than I can reach with my live seminars and my one-on-one coaching of sales superstars and soon-to-be sales superstars. Just in the time it takes me to fly to a seminar location, conduct a 2-day seminar for several hundred people and return home, Eric could conduct two or three webinars and reach 1,000 or more salespeople.

This book, combined with Eric's webinars, will present you with a bonanza of powerful sales ideas that you can put to immediate use to significantly increase your sales.

I wish you great success,

Donald Moine, Ph.D.
Marketing and Sales Psychologist
Personal Coach to Sales Superstars
President, Association for Human Achievement, Inc.
Palos Verdes, CA 90274
www.DrMoine.com

Introduction

Dear Friend,

For the past twenty years I have searched for the finest ideas on how to make more sales. My search started when I was about to be fired from my first sales job twenty years ago. Initially, I began (somewhat frantically, I might add!) looking for enough sales skills to keep my job.

Well, I'm happy to say that I did learn enough about sales to keep my job. In fact, with *proper training*, I realized I was very good at sales. I then devoted even more time, energy, and study to becoming the absolute best sales professional possible.

So how did I become a sales trainer? I had never had the goal to become a sales professional, let alone a sales trainer.

Sales training found me. When others at the company I was working for began to see and notice the amazing results I was producing, they started asking me questions like, "Eric, how are you able to produce these results?" I began sharing with them what was working for me. As a result, many of them saw huge increases in their own results. Suddenly, I found a new mission in life, one that still drives me to this day: ***to help other people make more sales***.

With this in mind, in 1998 I started Eric Lofholm International. Our purpose is to teach people how to make more sales. I am proud to say that we have become a great global training organization—we literally help people all over the world learn the finer skills of sales persuasion, success, and influence.

Now I have written *The System*. This book represents many of the best ideas I have learned, discovered, implemented, and shared over the last two decades. I am excited to share this material with you.

Who is this book for? Anyone who wants to make more sales. This includes traditional salespeople, real estate agents, loan officers, auto sales, insurance sales, financial advisors, coaches, consultants, network marketers, real estate investors, speakers, sales managers, VP of sales, and sales trainers. In fact, anyone who would like to learn the principles of influence will benefit from this material.

My Story

Okay, I know what many of you might be thinking right now. *Well, Eric, that's fine for you—you're a sales superstar. In fact, you were probably* born *a sales superstar. I'm just an average person trying to make a good living.* Or perhaps you're thinking, *Eric, selling comes easy to you. It doesn't for me.*

Starting out, was I any different than you? Let me tell you my story, and you decide.

I was very successful right out of high school. At my first job out of high school, I made over a hundred thousand...not dollars, mind you; I made over a hundred thousand *hamburgers*. I was literally a cook at McDonald's.

When I was a cook at McDonald's, I also attended a two-year community college. At least you were *supposed* to go for two years. I went to community college for five years, and still never received my two-year associate's degree.

So my life was headed nowhere. I was literally wandering aimlessly through life with no goals and no direction. Then I experienced a turning point. It came while attending a real estate investment seminar. Prior to attending, I was filled with hope and inspiration that I could go to this program and learn something that would make a significant difference in my life. And boy, was I right! I had no clue what was about to happen.

I went to this program believing in the possibility that something powerful could happen for me in my life. Then I met one of the speakers: Dante Perano. Dante was a multi-millionaire then and still is to this day. He made his money as a very successful global real estate investor.

Dante was there that day to share a powerful message with everyone about how to create wealth through real estate investing. As I sat listening in the audience, Dante made a statement that changed my life: "If you're willing to do the work, I will teach you what to do."

I had taken a day off at my job at McDonald's to attend this seminar, and even though Dante was talking to an audience of 300 people, I felt that his suggestion was aimed directly at me. Now, what he meant was, *When I've finished my presentation, go to the back table and purchase my home study course.* But that's not what I heard. We hear what we want to hear, and I distinctly heard Dante Perano pledge to personally mentor me.

Of course, Dante wasn't really extending an invitation to me to be my mentor! But when you want something badly enough, however, good things happen. Six months later, I became Dante's personal assistant. I quit my job at McDonald's and began traveling all over the country with a multi-millionaire.

You've probably heard that a big influence on how we think is the people we associate with. I didn't read that in a book, I lived it. I went from associating with college students and my McDonald's co-workers to rubbing shoulders with a real estate magnate. It shifted my entire way of thinking.

Dante offered me a part-time job as his assistant, but I needed to do something else with the remainder of my time, so he offered me a telemarketing position. A sales job! I never had any intention of being in sales. I just drifted into it because I wanted to be mentored by Dante.

I quickly discovered I was terrible at selling. I was the bottom producer on the team. At the end of my first year, I was put on quota probation. The quota was $10,000 a month in gross sales. I had missed quota two months in a row.

If you have ever struggled in sales before, I can understand and relate with you because that's where I was. My back was against the wall; I *had* to hit quota or lose my job...and be a failure. At the end of the day, in sales, you have to *know* how to sell. You have to know what to say, when to say it, how to close, how to handle objections, how to set appointments, how to build trust. These are all sales skills that you have to have to be successful, and I didn't have any.

You've probably heard the expression, "What is your why?" Well, my "why" was that I was newly married at the time. My wife Jarris and I got married on December 19, 1992. She was eighteen at the time, and I was twenty-two. We eloped at the Heart of Reno Chapel in Reno, Nevada.

We didn't invite her family and we didn't invite my family. When we showed up at the chapel, the staff asked if we had a witness for the ceremony. We said, "No. It's just us." They marked the box "rent a witness." We had to pay an extra twenty-five dollars to rent a witness to make the ceremony legal.

At Christmas time, my wife Jarris went to see her family and I went to see mine. When she told her family that she had gotten married, their response was, "Really? Who'd you marry?" Jarris replied, "Remember that guy I was dating who worked at McDonald's? The one who went to community college for five years and never graduated? That's your new son-in-law!" You can imagine her family's reaction.

Well, fast-forward a year later. I'm about to get fired from my job. I can't imagine facing my in-laws after having gotten off on such a bad foot with them. I had a very real problem: I didn't know how to sell. So I did the only thing that I could think to do. I prayed about it.

My prayers were answered when the number one sales mind in the world, Dr. Donald Moine, came into my life and began to mentor and coach me. Dr. Moine is the author of *Unlimited Selling Power*, which *Success* magazine called the best book ever written on the subject of professional selling. I affectionately call Dr. Moine the Obi-Wan Kenobi (Luke Skywalker's mentor in *Star Wars*) of sales training. Dr. Moine took me under his wing and began to mentor and coach me. With Dr. Moine's help, my results increased. In my make-or-break month, I had sales of $10,500, making quota by $500. The following month, I did $51,000 in gross sales! Seven months later, I did $160,000 in gross sales in a single month!

Please read and remember this phrase:

Selling is a learned skill.

Selling is a learned skill. I learned how to sell, and sell very successfully. Best of all, I can teach you to do the same.

Your Investment

How is this book different from other sales books?

Most sales books talk about sales techniques or sales mindset. In this book, I will share with you the best sales techniques that I have discovered, as well as how to sell by serving others. I will share with you how to become a sales champion by selling from honesty, integrity and compassion. You will experience a whole new way of thinking about the sales profession. This new paradigm will help you create real sales breakthroughs.

I understand that you will spend time, money, and energy with the material in this book. Will your investment be worth it? Yes! I can confidently say that this book could quite possibly be the *most profitable* book you will ever read. If I were to charge you the fair market value for the ideas presented in this book, your cost would be roughly $10,000. And at $10,000 you would still be getting a bargain.

Let's be realistic, though. As powerful as the content is in this book is, very few people would be willing to pay $10,000 for it. Still, I want to encourage you to treat this book *as if you invested $10,000 for it.* By treating *The System* this way, you are sure to sharpen your salesmanship *and* boost your sales as a direct result of the ideas in this book.

Getting the Most Out of This Book

I suggest you *study* this book rather than simply just read it. Use a notebook to create a Success Journal where you can record the best ideas you learn from this book and how you're applying them. To help you get started, I've included a Success Journal Notes section at the end of this book with blank pages where you can record the best ideas you learn from each chapter and the best ideas you learn from the book as a whole. As you read, identify the ten best ideas you pick up from reading and record them for quick reference at the end of your Success Journal Notes. (And I left extra lines, so don't worry if you want to write more than ten!)

I have read sections of some of my favorite books numerous times. The reason for this is because I get more out of what the author has to share each time I review it. I suggest that you read over and over again the chapters or sections of the sales process where you need the most help.

To reflect the three top ways you can elevate your sales results, I have divided the book into three parts:

Part I: Inner Game

Part II: Outer Game

Part III: Action

The inner game is the mental side of selling. It is your beliefs, your comfort zone, how you deal with rejection.

The outer game is the tactical side of selling: What you say, when you say it, how you say it.

The third component is action, which focuses on moving yourself to follow through and take action on what you know you should be doing.

While each chapter can be read on its own, *The System* does follow a logical sequence. You can skip to the chapter you need the most help with, or read the book in sequence.

Here are additional thoughts on how to elevate your results from this material:

- Each chapter can be read as a stand-alone chapter.
- Over time, you will want to read the book completely a total of seven times.
- If you are working on referrals, read that chapter once per day for seven days.
- *Believe* that this book will make you money. (In fact, believe that this book will make you more money than any book you have ever read.)
- Mark the best ideas you encounter with a highlighter or jot them down in your journal notes.
- The fair price for the information you will learn from this book is $10,000. I want you to read the book as if you paid $10,000 for it.
- This book changes people's lives. As you are reading it, think about the people you care about who you will want to give a copy of this book to.

A Final Note

Before we get started let me share with you a powerful metaphor about how to create possible breakthroughs with your selling.

Imagine a circle. Now imagine a small slice of that pie that represents 3% of the circle. The circle is all the knowledge that exists in the world. The 3% pie slice represents things that you know you know. (For example, you know you are reading *The System*. You know you know your phone number.)

Next, imagine a pie slice that is 7% of the circle. The 7% represents things that you know you don't know. (For example, you probably know you don't know how to fly an airplane.)

That leaves the remaining 90% of the pie. This 90% are the things you don't know you don't know. In other words, this is the unknown realm for you. When you move from the you-don't-know-you-don't-know to the known realm, it creates a *breakthrough possibility*. This book is about sharing ideas, strategies, and concepts that will help you create many breakthroughs in your sales results.

Key Points

I want to share a secret with you. Many of the success stories in this book happened because the person created an intention to be one of my success stories. I encourage you to create an intention right now to become one of my success stories—a person that I will talk about in one of my future books, future audio programs, or seminars. And if you are willing to create that intention, I want you to write it down in your Success Journal Notes at the end of this book right now. Then send me an email at **wins@ericlofholm.com** and declare your new intention to be one of my success stories. This may be one of the most important action items for you in the entire book.

Some of you reading this book know me from my seminars. Others are meeting me for the very first time. I want to acknowledge you for being a person of action. Just by reading this book you are declaring your intention to become better at sales and influence. I want to give a special welcome to those readers who are meeting me for the first time. Thank you for having faith that I can help you and for believing it is possible that I can share something with you that can make a difference for you in your life and your sales results.

Let's begin!

To your success,
Eric Lofholm

PART I

The Inner Game
of Selling

Sales greatness starts with the mindset that you can become great.

—Eric Lofholm

Part I of this book focuses on the sales *mindset*.

Most people in our world today think negatively about sales. For example, when you think about selling, what do you think of? The most common answers that come to mind are negative: arm twisting, high pressure, manipulation, like a used car salesman, and so on. This negative thinking creates a tremendous challenge for the person selling. If you have a negative view about sales and you go into your sales presentation with that mindset, that mindset will act as an imaginary hurdle that's going to prevent you from achieving your potential.

Here I'm going to share with you the mindset of a true sales champion. My definition of selling is this: *Selling equals service*. When you sell, sell from honesty, integrity, and compassion. It is not about a hard sell, it is about a *heart* sell. Selling is about leading and moving people to action. This paragraph is extremely important. In my life seminars I have my students write it down in their notes word for word. I then give them the instruction to say these words to themselves or out loud ten times per day for the next thirty days. I will give you the same instruction. First highlight the paragraph. Then start saying the paragraph to yourself ten times per day for the next thirty days. Move at the speed of instruction.

Please note that this short introduction to Part I is one of the most important points in the book. By reading this paragraph ten times per day for thirty days you will have said *selling equals service* to yourself 300 times. Change begins in language. If I could make you believe this one thing—that *selling equals service*—this alone would probably double your sales.

Chapter 1

Sales Mindset

In this section we are going to talk about the Inner Game of selling. Please note that to get the most out of the techniques and strategies mentioned later in this book, *it is valuable to first develop your sales mindset*. This, then, is an extremely important section of the book.

When you think of a salesperson, what do you think of? The most common responses I receive from my live seminar audiences are things like this: arm-twisting, high pressure, manipulation, used car salesman, selfish.

Have you heard this joke: How do you know when a salesperson is lying? *His lips are moving.*

I want you to imagine Santa Claus. Santa Claus, of course, has his bag of toys. And as he goes from house to house, he carries his bag around with him. Well, we carry around our beliefs with us just like Santa Claus carries around that bag of toys.

Most people have a negative view about sales. A large part of this is our cultural hypnosis. Hypnosis is simply the non-critical acceptance of an idea. In other words, most people *believe* the negative beliefs about sales and salespeople because that is what our culture tells us—not because it is true.

Now, for millions of people who need effective sales skills—like salespeople, coaches, consultants, network marketers, entrepreneurs, and so on—*they have negative views on selling, too*. They carry that negative view with them from presentation to presentation. This mindset manifests itself in a salesperson being a weak closer or, even worse, not even asking for the order in the first place. Instead of powerfully asking for the order, many people say, "Here's my business card; call me when you are ready to move forward."

This "call me when you're ready" approach, of course, simply doesn't work. I define selling this way:

Selling equals service.

When you sell, sell from honesty, integrity, and compassion. It is not about a *hard* sell; it is about a *heart* sell. Professional salespeople simply lead prospects and move others to action, *action which benefits the prospect/client.* The close is simply the natural conclusion to a well-delivered sales presentation.

Your subconscious mind wants to keep "you" consistent with your identity. One way to identify your identity is to listen to yourself talk. Listen especially carefully to whatever follows the word "I." When you say "I," you are probably taking that belief on as your identity or as your mental picture of yourself (self-image).

"I am not good at sales."

"I'm not good at closing."

"I'm not good at recruiting."

"I hate selling."

"I don't like the phone."

Salespeople make these statements all the time. Listen to yourself talk and pay attention to whatever follows the word "I."

Here's a quick story that illustrates the power of identity. Many years ago I was asked to give a motivational talk at a homeless shelter. Mary Mahy was the executive director of Harvest for the Hungry, located in Pacific Beach, California. Mary was homeless herself at one point. She now dedicates her time to helping others who face the same challenge. Mary created a special lunch. Anyone who lived on the streets was invited. I went to that meeting all excited about sharing some great ideas to motivate and inspire the group. Perhaps one person in the audience would rent a room, or get a job. Maybe even one person in the audience would one day become a homeowner.

I gave my presentation with lots of enthusiasm that day. When it was over, I went up to one of the gentlemen from the audience and said conversationally, "What's it like being homeless?"

He looked at me like I was nuts. He said, "What are you talking about?"

"I'm just curious," I replied. "What's it like being homeless?"

He goes, "Homeless? I'm not homeless."

I said, "You're not?"

"No," he said. "I just live outdoors."

He wasn't saying it to be funny; he was serious. His self-image, his mental picture of himself, was not of him being a homeless person; he was simply someone who lived outdoors. He had no motivation to rent a room, get an apartment, or buy property.

Again, your identity drives your behavior. Do you view yourself as a middle-of-the-pack salesperson? Do you see yourself as a Dow Jones salesperson, someone who is up and down? Do you see yourself as someone who is very consistent? Do you see yourself as a top producer? Do you see yourself becoming a top producer?

What you envision happening is very important in terms of the overall results that you will eventually achieve.

The Law of Belief

You can reprogram the subconscious mind for success by using the Law of Belief: whatever you tell yourself over and over and over again, you will eventually believe. Start affirming to yourself that *selling equals service*. When you sell, sell from honesty, integrity, and compassion. In order for you to achieve sales greatness it may require that you change the way you view yourself. Start viewing yourself as a sales champion. Create an expectation on yourself that you are going to become great in sales.

Here's a quick story about one of my star clients, Joey Aszterbaum, a loan officer. While attending one of my one-day sales seminars, Joey said, "I am not good at time management."

I responded, "I believe you. If you say you're not good, then you're not good."

Change begins in *language*. Speak as if what you are saying is the truth. Speak into existence what it is that you want.

I said, "Joey, if you want to become good at time management, then speak that. If you want to become a time management master, then speak that. The Law of Belief is simply that whatever you tell yourself over and over and over again, you will eventually believe."

Well, Joey started affirming that he is a time management master. I taught him to affirm it three ways:

I am a time management master.

He is a time management master.

And then your name: *Joey is a time management master.*

I told Joey to tell himself this over and over and over again. In doing this, he literally reprogrammed his subconscious mind for success. Napoleon Hill, in his book *Think and Grow Rich*, calls this autosuggestion. I call it repeated affirmation.

Think of the famous commercial for Rolaids. How do you spell "relief"? R-O-L-A-I-D-S. How did Rolaids get that into our subconscious? Repetition. They bombarded our subconscious minds over and over and over again. Again, this is why I want you to read the book seven times through, to really understand what I am trying to teach you here.

Back to Joey. He says his affirmations over and over. And wouldn't you know it, he starts to get really good at time management. One day he was meeting with a real estate agent, who said, "Joey, you're so good at time management. How are you able to do all that you do?"

And Joey simply said, "It's easy. I am a time management master." That's what came to Joey's mind. He literally reprogrammed his subconscious mind for success.

Born with Greatness?

So you want to become a true sales professional? A master influencer? Great! First, imagine what that would mean to you. Power. Prestige. Success. Wealth. Great relationships with the people that you care about most. Each of these and more are available to you when you learn how to become a master influencer.

I know this to be true because this is the life that I'm living right now. As I mentioned in the Introduction, this wasn't always the case. I wasn't born with these skills; influence, like all skills, has to be learned. Yes, it is true that we are born with a certain level of persuasiveness, and some are born more persuasive than others. But for you to reach your potential, you must develop your skills.

Michael Jordan, one of the greatest basketball players of all time, became that way not because he was born that way. Each summer, Jordan worked on his game. He became great over time, not because he was born that way, but because of the training he received.

Michael Jordan was born with the potential to become great.

I was born with the potential to become great.

You were born with the potential to become great.

In order for the greatness to come out, you must be trained. This book, *The System*, is simply one step (I like to think it's a critical step!) to helping you become a master influencer.

One of my mentors is Tony Robbins. Tony is one of the most exceptional seminar leaders of all time! I watched video footage of him early in his career and, although he was very effective, his skills when he first started are nowhere *near* where they are today. He developed his skills over time.

You've got to work to make yourself a great salesperson. It takes time.

Want another example? You've probably had this experience: You're driving in your car listening to your favorite song on the radio, and you begin to sing along with the words to the song.

My question for you is this: When did you set a goal to learn the words to the song? Of course, the answer is you never did. Well, then, how did you then learn the words to the song? By repetition.

Embracing Selling

Let's discuss a little more the negative connotations associated with selling. To overcome these negatives and become a master influencer, we must instead *embrace* selling. Now, the thought of embracing selling may cause you to cringe, and the reason why is obvious—again, all those negative connotations floating around in the world we live in. Think about how salespeople are portrayed in the media, such as in movies like *Glengarry Glen Ross*. It's no wonder people resist selling.

Let me ask you a question, though. What if that isn't what selling is? What if selling is really about helping people? What if selling was about serving others? About being honest? About making a difference in the world? Would you be willing to embrace selling then? What if the idea of selling was the key to you reaching your dreams, your potential?

There is nothing more powerful than a good idea whose time has come. Maybe your entire career you resisted selling and today's your day! Today's your day to embrace the skill that can take you to that next level of success.

You see, selling is *not* about high pressure. It's *not* about manipulation. It's *not* about being selfish. It's *not* about arm-twisting. No, I teach you to sell from honesty, integrity, and compassion. I am *proud* to be in sales. Why? Because selling skills are the key, in my opinion, to having everything that you want in your life. I'm able to enjoy the finer things in life by focusing on helping others. I'm able to get what I want, not by focusing on me, but by focusing on serving.

I'm serving you right now. I am providing you far more value than the cover price of this book. This is the key to financial success—providing more value to somebody else than what they're paying for your products or service.

If you look at the most successful companies in the world, this is how they create wealth and success. Think about companies like Walmart, Starbucks, Toyota, McDonald's. They focus on providing value. They're all very financially successful, yet the wealth they created is a byproduct or a side effect to adding value.

A few years ago I met Garrett Gunderson. Garrett helps people in the financial world. Garrett has built a very successful business by focusing on adding value to others. His website is **http://www.garrettbgunderson.com/**.

Another name for this is the *precessional effect*, a concept explored very effectively in Jack Canfield's highly recommended book, *The Success Principles*. The actual definition of a precessional effect is *bodies in motion affecting bodies in motion*. It's simply a side effect to you taking action. You see, when you take action towards a goal, there's a side effect to you taking that action.

Let me share a quick story with you. One of my clients, Debbie Severn, purchased one of my *How to Master the Art of Goal Setting* audio programs on CD. (Just like with this book, I encourage listeners to listen to the audio programs seven times.) So, being a good student, Debbie listens to my goal setting series while driving her then ten-year-old son, Eric, to and from soccer practice and football practice and to school. To Eric, I'm known as the goal-setting guy.

Now, her son wanted to get a video game. When he asked his mom to buy the game for him, Debbie replied, "I am not going to buy the video game for you. Remember all those goal-setting CDs we've been listening to? Well, why don't you set a *goal* to get the video game."

This goal was no small talk. Eric needed to get $30 by Friday night at 5:00 p.m. and today was Wednesday.

Instead of buying the video game for her ten-year-old, she taught him goal setting with my help through those audio CDs. And, most importantly, Eric ended up getting the video game.

Don't you wish somebody had taught you goal setting at the tender age of ten? I know I wish somebody had taught me. I didn't learn until I was in my twenties. That's the precessional effect: Debbie's son Eric learning goal setting. She bought the CDs and listened to them for her own personal development in her business. It was never a goal for her son to learn goal setting. It just happened. It was a side effect to action.

This concept dates back to a gentleman named Buckminster Fuller (1895-1983), the architect and designer perhaps best known as the inventor of the geodesic dome. Fuller called this a *generalized principle* that works in every case. It's like a natural law—it's always happening. Precession is happening around us every day. (This subject will be discussed in more depth in Chapter 2.)

Most salespeople focus on their commission, hitting the numbers, making money, hitting quota, and paying their bills, with the side effect of helping some people. This is all backwards! What I teach is instead to focus on adding value; then as a byproduct, or a side effect, or a precessional effect, we're able to create financial success for ourselves.

Why do salespeople focus on the numbers and their commission and quota? That's what they were taught. Why? Well, the majority of the sales training that happens in the world today is *not* done by a professional trainer like me. The majority of the sales training done on a global level—there are millions of salespeople out there—is done on the branch level, from their sales manager.

How does a sales manager become a sales manager? In most cases, this usually happens by default. However, this isn't true in every case, as there are some incredible sales managers out there that are wonderful at managing. But the reality is that many managers out there became a manager by default. The sales manager got promoted, quit, got fired, transferred, or went back into sales, and all of a sudden the company needs a new sales manager. Bingo, you're it!

Then the vice president of sales comes in and says, "By the way, get me the numbers." So now you're now the sales manager and all you've learned to say to your team is "get me the numbers." It's not some manager's fault and it's not the salesperson's fault. Everybody's doing the best that they can. The salespeople are doing the best that they can and the managers are doing the best that they can.

Here's another example. Looking back on how you grew up, do you sometimes wish your parents had raised you a little bit differently? Probably, but you also realize that they did the best they could. After all, when you were born, you didn't come with an instruction manual! So, all of these managers all over the world, some were never trained on the concepts that we're talking about today. They simply said, "Get the numbers."

I know when I started in selling, that's what I focused on. Why? Because that's what my manager told me. But now I'm sharing with you a new view: a different way of looking at it. It's a way that can help you reach levels of success you may have never even imagined.

Influencing others is, at the highest level, really about showing the person how they can benefit from doing whatever you're asking them to do.

Whether you're attempting to influence your children to clean up their room or attempting to influence a prospect to buy from you, you want to bring them back. Regardless of the type of influence that you want to have, it's all about focusing on that individual and how you can add value to them by getting them to follow through on whatever it is that you're representing.

So here's the key idea: Embrace selling by focusing on adding value, and as a side effect to you adding value, you'll create success for yourself.

How the Mind Works

In order for you to achieve your potential, you must think like a master of influence. I want to talk with you now about some of the ways that your brain works.

You have a conscious part of your brain. You also have a subconscious part of your brain. I want you to imagine an iceberg. If the tip of that iceberg, the part above the surface of the water, represents 10% of the total iceberg, then 90% of that iceberg lies beneath the surface. When you use the iceberg as a metaphor to describe your conscious brain and your subconscious brain, we say that the conscious part of your brain is that top 10%, and the subconscious part of your brain is the 90% beneath the surface. If this is true, then what's really driving your behavior—the conscious part of your brain, or the subconscious part?

Of course, the answer is the subconscious part of your brain. We all have beliefs on a subconscious level that prevents us from achieving our potential.

Here are some examples of those beliefs:

I'm not good enough.

I'm not good at sales.

I'm not worth it.

I hate the phone.

I'm not good at recruiting.

These beliefs take root on a subconscious level. The goal of this section is to reprogram your subconscious mind to think like a master of influence. How do you do this? Again, use positive affirmations to "state" what you want to have happen.

Several years ago I did a training session for Sabastiani Vineyards and Winery in Sonoma, California. I shared some ideas on how beliefs affect performance. When the session was done the manager that hired me pulled me aside and shared one of the best stories I have ever heard about beliefs. The manager, a graduate of East Carolina University, told me a story about a football game between that school and North Carolina State. This particular year East Carolina had a quarterback that went on to start in the National Football League. His name was Jeff Blake. They also had a running back named Tony Collins, who made it to the NFL as well. East Carolina ended up playing North Carolina State in the Peach Bowl that year.

Now in college football, often all of the fans from one team will sit in the same section of the stadium. That was true on this day. Twenty thousand East Carolina fans all sat in the same section of the stadium.

East Carolina had a terrible time. They were getting dominated, losing 34-9 with seven minutes to go in the game. If you're playing in a football game, you're down twenty-five points, and you're being dominated in the game, what's typically the end result of the game? Of course, you're going to lose.

One guy in the East Carolina section had the power of belief. He stood up and began to chant, "We believe! We believe! We believe!" Now keep in mind this was the fourth quarter and who knows how many beers he had had by this point. At first, no one joined in. But then a couple of people began chanting too. Then a few more. The next thing you know, all 20,000 East Carolina fans begin to chant, "We believe! We believe! We believe!" Oh, yeah—East Carolina, in the last seven minutes of that game, scored four unanswered touchdowns to win the game!

Never underestimate the *power of belief.*

What you believe about selling is critical to your success.

I have a younger brother named Andrew. As a youth, he played Little League baseball. When his coach found out that I used to be a motivational speaker for Tony Robbins, the coach asked me if I'd be willing to come in and do a motivational talk. Even at the Little League level, it's very competitive, especially with parents.

I said I'd love to. I began thinking, "What can I share with a group of twelve- and thirteen-year-olds that can make a difference?"

One of the stories I told Andrew's team I just shared with you—the East Carolina-NC State "We Believe" story. Andrew's team loved the story. In fact— and I didn't tell them to do this—anytime they were up to bat in the fourth, fifth or sixth inning and the other team was ahead, they would chant from the dugout: "We believe! We believe! We believe!"

An amazing thing happened. They led the league that year in come-from-behind victories. They played a team that hadn't lost in a year a half and beat them. They not only won the League, they won the year-end tournament, too.

Never underestimate the *power of belief.*

Earl Nightingale, the motivational speaker often called "the dean of personal development," once said, "We become what we think about."

You see, if you see yourself as somebody who becomes successful, then you'll become that. If you see yourself as somebody who is a master of influence, then you will become that.

You can literally reprogram your subconscious mind for success utilizing the power of belief and affirmations. I've used them. They've made a tremendous difference in my life, and I'm speaking to you as somebody who was a former cook at McDonald's, spent five years in community college, and never graduated.

I would like to share with you some of my favorite affirmation. I say affirmations regularly. I change the affirmations based on what is important to me in life. Here's a few of them:

- Each day I am wiser.

- I am stronger from every experience that I have.

- I am enjoying the "now."
- I now have all the money I need to do everything that I want.
- All of my investments are profitable.
- People love to buy from me.
- People love to give me referrals.
- I effortlessly attract success.
- I have everything that I need in order to create the life that I want.
- I create my reality.
- I love God.
- I have all the time that I need to do everything that I want.
- I attract world-class people who want to be on my team.

Use my affirmations as a template to create your own.

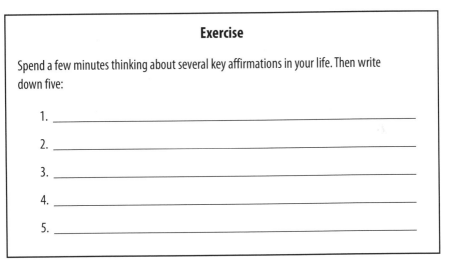

Exercise

Spend a few minutes thinking about several key affirmations in your life. Then write down five:

1. _____

2. _____

3. _____

4. _____

5. _____

The Frog and the Scorpion

Would you like to double your income? I want to share with you an exercise that I walk many of my clients through. Many of them have taken this exact exercise and literally doubled their income.

This is a story about a woman named Jandee. I was on a coaching call with Jandee, who at the time was a newbie in the loan business. I asked her, "Jandee, how much money do you believe that you can make in a month?"

Let me ask you right now—How much money do you believe that you can make in a month? Whatever the answer is, write it down here:

I believe I can make _____ **_per month._**

Jandee said, "Five thousand dollars."

"Okay, Jandee," I replied. "Now take that number and double it."

So what I'd like _you_ to do right now, take the number you wrote down, double it, and write this number here:

I believe I can make _____ **_per month._**

Jandee said, "Ten thousand dollars."

I said, "Jandee, tell yourself that you're going to earn ten thousand dollars in the next thirty days."

So she did that. Now, you tell yourself that you're going to earn your new doubled amount in the next thirty days.

I said, "Jandee, what did the little voice in the back of your head tell you when you told yourself that you were going to earn that doubled amount in the next thirty days?"

Jandee smiled knowingly and replied, "It said you're crazy! Not in this lifetime. Yeah, right. You would have been lucky to earn five thousand."

You know you have a voice in the back of your head too, right? That little voice speaks to you at up to five hundred words a minute.

Now, as I just said that to you, you might have been thinking to yourself, "What's Eric talking about? I don't have a voice in the back of my head that talks to me up to five hundred words a minute."

That's the voice that I'm talking about! You might have seen the movie _What Women Want_ with Mel Gibson, where Mel walks by women and he can hear their inner thoughts. We all have a little voice in the back of our head that speaks to us at up to five hundred words a minute. Well, Jandee's voice said, _Not in this lifetime, you'll never make ten thousand in a month,_ and so on.

The Law of Belief is whatever you tell yourself over and over and over again, you will eventually believe. I told Jandee this: "Speak this new idea of making $10,000 into existence. Embrace the Law of Belief. Jandee, write it on an index card. I want you to tell yourself over and over and over again that you'll earn ten thousand dollars in the next thirty days."

Thirty days pass and guess what happened. Nothing! Sixty days passed, though, and she made a little over ten thousand dollars!

About six months after Jandee's breakthrough I called her on the phone and asked her how she was doing. We started talking. I asked her point-blank how much money had she made last month.

"I made, um, thirty-three last month."

"You only made thirty-three hundred?"

"No, Eric. I made thirty-three thousand!"

This is six months after she believed five thousand dollars was a lot of money in a month!

So, I want you to take that new doubled amount. Speak it into existence and watch the income miracle happen for you. Part of the purpose of your subconscious mind is to keep you consistent with your identity. One way to help you determine your identity is to start listening to how you describe yourself to others when you use the word "I." Know that when you use the word "I," you may be creating an identity belief that will drive you on a subconscious level. Here are some examples:

> I am not good at sales.
>
> I am not good at time management.
>
> I am always late.

I want to share another quick story to demonstrate the power of identity. It's a famous story about the scorpion and the frog.

There's a scorpion that wants to get to the other side of the river but he doesn't know how to swim. He sees a frog and, knowing the frog can swim, asks the frog to transport him across the river on his back. The frog says no.

The scorpion says, "Why can't you help me?"

And the frog says, "Because scorpions sting frogs, and I don't want you to sting me, Mister Scorpion."

Well, this particular scorpion was a very persuasive scorpion. He convinced the frog that he wouldn't kill him. So the scorpion gets on the frog's back and they start swimming across the river. They get about midway across the river and, wouldn't you know it, the scorpion stings the frog.

As the frog is drowning, the frog looks up at the scorpion and says, "Mister Scorpion! Why did you sting me? I'm about to drown. I'm going to be killed. You're going to be killed. Why'd you do that?"

The scorpion replies, "Because that's what scorpion's do—they sting frogs."

Even though it meant death to the scorpion and the frog, the scorpion had to stay consistent with his identity of itself.

Do you know why you drive the car you drive? Why you wear the clothes you wear? Earn the income that you earn? Live in the house that you live in? One reason why is because that's how you view yourself. You view yourself as somebody that's at the level of success that you're currently at.

I can almost hear you screaming, "But Eric I'm not earning the income of my dreams! I'm not driving my dream car! What are you talking about?"

What I'm talking about is we become what our self-image is. Part of the purpose of this part of your brain is to keep you consistent with your identity. A master influencer attracts into their life whatever they want. They earn the income of their dreams. They drive the car of their dreams. They have great relationships. They make a tremendous difference in the world. If you start viewing yourself as a master of influence, then that's what you will become.

Every Day a TEN!

I have one last concept regarding mindset that I want to share with you. It's really made a big difference to me and I believe it can make a big difference for you. When I speak in front of a group, I wear a pin that says "Ten." This is a philosophy; it's a way of being for peak performers.

Here's how I demonstrate living life on a level ten. When I teach my public seminars, I say, "Good morning." Everyone then says "good morning" back at a level six, in terms of energy and enthusiasm on a scale of one to ten, with ten being the best.

We do this again, only this time we're going to play at a level eight—a little more energy and a little more enthusiasm. "Good morning, everyone!"

Everyone roars back, "Good morning!" at a level eight.

Then we do it one last time, at a level ten. I want you to do it this time as if your success this year is riding on how much energy and enthusiasm you exude.

Okay, let's give it a try: "Good morning, everyone!"

Everyone roars back, including you, "Good morning, Eric!" at a level ten.

Now, the first time we do this, you played to the six. And the last time you did, you played at a ten.

Here's my question for you: Over the past thirty days, as you've been doing your business on a daily basis, what level have you been playing at? What level have you been playing at in terms of attitude and enthusiasm? What level have you been playing at in making the calls necessary for you to be successful? During the past thirty days, what level have you been playing at in terms of action?

The level-ten metaphor goes far beyond your business—it ripples back to all areas of your life. During the past thirty days, what level have you been playing at in your health? What level have you been playing at in the relationships with the people that you care about most? Your children? Your spouse? Your significant other? The people you care about most?

Over the last thirty days, what level have you been playing at spiritually?

Because my belief is that you get out of life what you put into it, and all of the rewards are for those that play full-out, then who decides what level we play at on a daily basis? The answer is, *we do.*

John Wooden, the great former coach of the UCLA Bruins basketball team, has another way of describing the level-ten mindset. It goes like this: He never focused on winning; instead, he focused on getting the best out of his players. In fact, he *demanded* the best out of his players! It wasn't whether you won or lost. Because in every game, such as basketball, there's always a winner and there's a loser. But Wooden, you see, taught his players that—in basketball *and* in life—your focus should be all about effort, not winning and losing. And that resonates with me.

You see, you go out on a sales presentation and you either make the sale or you don't. A lot of people deliver their presentation, don't make the sale, get back in their car, and feel sorry for themselves, when in reality they did everything right.

The purpose of a sales presentation is not to make a sale! **The purpose of a sales presentation is to deliver a quality presentation and ask for the order if your product or service adds value to the prospect.** Your job is to deliver a quality presentation. If you do enough of those, then everything else takes care of itself.

One day I was listening to a radio interview with a celebrated Major League Baseball player. The interviewer asked the player if it upset him when he hits the ball perfectly and it goes right to the second baseman the entire game. The athlete replied that it didn't, and why should it? He did his job. His job is to have a quality at bat. Your job is to deliver a quality sales presentation.

Embrace this philosophy of giving it your personal best. Best of all, you will know if you've been giving it your best in life. So, what I can share with you from personal experience is that the universe rewards people who take action differently than those who don't. There's a whole new level of success that's available to you if you would just simply make a decision right now, this moment, to live from this day forward according to the philosophy of John Wooden of playing at a level ten.

Level 7+

We can't play at a level 10 all the time. Another way of saying this is, you can't sprint a marathon. Consistency is one of the keys to long-term success. My intention is to play at a 7+ everyday. I believe that if you play at a 7+ for a month that is equal to a level 10 month!

Ideas Into Action

Many years ago, I was trained by my mentor, Dr. Donald Moine. Dr. Moine is, in my opinion, the world's greatest sales mind. Of course, eventually I was going to become great in sales—after all, I was being trained by Dr Moine. Well, you're being trained by me. Through this book you are associating with me. And I want you to encourage you to create an expectation on yourself that you will become great in sales. We get what we expect to get.

Key Points Review

- Selling = Service
- Law of Belief: what you tell yourself over and over eventually comes true
- Create a list of positive affirmations for all parts of your life
- Embrace selling
- Live full-out, called Level 10
- Play at a 7+ consistently

Chapter 2

What I Learned from One of the World's Greatest Thinkers

This chapter reveals the success secret of one of the world's greatest thinkers. The secret is a principle called precession. Here how's I was introduced to it.

A number of years ago, I attended a seminar called "Money & You." Jonathan Dune, one of my mentors, had been encouraging me to attend this program for more than two years. Because of Jonathan's commitment, I attended the program with my wife.

Wow—it was a life-changing experience. The program featured the work of Buckminster Fuller, whose ideals for using the world's resources with maximum purpose at the least waste earned him wealth and fame as one of the greatest thinkers of the twentieth century. Although I never personally met Fuller, I have been greatly influenced by his work through the "Money & You" seminar. (I highly recommend this seminar. To learn more, visit **www.excellerated.com**.)

One of the principles taught in the "Money & You" seminar was *precession*, which I had never heard of prior to attending the seminar. I have been able to benefit from this principle ever since.

The Power of Precession

Precession is a generalized principle, one that works in every case. It doesn't work some of the time, it doesn't work most of the time. It works *all* of the time. It's like gravity. On our Earth, gravity is always working. Precession can be defined this way: bodies in motion affecting bodies in motion. I like to think of it another way, as the side effects resulting from a particular action. When you take an action to reach a goal, this action creates a ripple effect of often-unexpected side effects. Why is this important?

> *The universe rewards people who take action differently than those who don't.*

Often when I learn something new, I look at what I learned from a sales perspective. The lens I look through in life is a sales lens. (For example, my wife Jarris was a referral. I am probably the only person in the world that says he met his wife through a referral!) Here's my interpretation of precession as it relates to helping you create a sales breakthrough. Pay close attention to what I am about to share with you. **This is one of the five most profound ideas I have ever learned.** (Incidentally, the previous sentence is an example of an advanced scripting technique called an ICR: an Interest Creating Remark. To make your sales presentation more interesting, sprinkle ICRs throughout the presentation. These are statements designed to let the prospect know you are about to share something important.) This is a great section of the book to review a minimum of seven times.

When you take action towards a goal, it creates a precession effect. During their sales presentation many salespeople focus on what they're going to get out of the presentation. Their goal is to close the sale, make the commission, win the trip, or hit quota. While those are worthy goals, they have no place in the sales presentation. The sales presentation instead *should be completely focused on adding value to the customer.*

This is one of my philosophies about sales. It is the highest level of influence that I know: to focus on adding value to the customer. Oftentimes, sales managers train their sales reps to focus on the money, and I believe that this is the wrong message. Numbers are important. The purpose of a fig tree is to grow figs, and if a fig tree does not grow figs the only thing it is good for is firewood.

The purpose of a sales professional is to produce sales. So we must produce, but this is a conversation about who we are *being* in the sales presentation, not the results we produce. This has everything to do with influence.

The Value Association

Greatness in sales comes by focusing on adding value to the customer. If you focus on the money you are going to make, the customer can intuitively pick that up. We've all been sold to by a salesperson that was focusing on the money, and we sensed it. And we still might have bought from that salesperson because we wanted what they were offering, not because the salesperson was focusing on the money. Tony Robbins would call this a "false neuro-association." Here's a good example of a false neuro-association. Say a baby lying on a sofa suddenly falls off onto a green carpet. The first thing the baby sees is the green carpet. Because the baby is hurt and starts crying, it might link up in its brain that "green carpet" equals "pain." That is a false neuro-association. The green carpet doesn't cause the pain; it's landing on the hard ground that causes pain. But the baby doesn't realize this.

Often times a salesperson will have a false neuro-association. They concentrate on their own personal goals. That may be causing their motivation, but that's not what's causing their sales success. They are achieving success despite the fact they are focusing on their own personal goals. Now I am not down on personal goals. I am all for you having the goal to become the top producer if that's what you desire; to get your dream car; to own the house of your dreams. Personal goals are wonderful things. I just believe they have no place in the sales process, especially in the sales presentation. I have a personal goal to purchase a second home in Lake Tahoe. As you are reading this book right now, you don't care whether I achieve that goal or not. You want to learn ideas in this book that are going to transform your life financially through selling.

Instead of focusing on what you can get out of the sales presentation, I want you to focus on adding value to the customer. When you focus on adding value to the customer, a precession effect happens, which is that you make the sale. You earn the income. You win the trip. You get your dream car—whatever is important to you. So you can create sales as a precession effect of you adding value. I call this the "Dr. Phil" way to success.

Most likely you know of Dr. Phil McGraw, the insanely popular television personality, psychologist, and author. Years back, however, he was not a household name. Oprah Winfrey helped Dr. Phil become famous. Oprah hired Dr. Phil when a Texas cattlemen's association was suing her. The Texans had a "beef" with Oprah. During a show about Mad Cow disease, Oprah said a guest's comments about cows being ground up and fed back to other cows "has just stopped me cold from eating another burger!" Of course, when Oprah talks, people listen, and according to the cattlemen's association, her remark decreased beef sales nationally. Oprah had to go to Texas to defend herself.

The cattle industry is a huge part of the Texas economy. Who knows, the judge in the case might even have belonged to the same country club as the attorney for the cattlemen's association. Oprah Winfrey, as you know, is an African American from a big city, Chicago. So with a wealthy African American city slicker down in Texas defending herself, under those circumstances anything could happen. Wisely, Oprah hired Dr. Phil as an advisor. Now there are many people whom, when they meet Oprah Winfrey, have the sole intention of getting on her show. This becomes their focus. I'm sure that Oprah has her guard up for people trying to take advantage of her like that.

Dr. Phil, though, focused on adding value to Oprah Winfrey. In fact, in one of Dr. Phil's books, he describes a time during the trial when he had to be brutally honest with her. This was probably unusual behavior for most people in Oprah's life, as they most likely tell her what she wants to hear. Dr. Phil was honest with her. And in doing so, he was focusing on adding value. Out of Dr. Phil focusing on adding value, as a precession effect Oprah Winfrey invited Dr Phil to be on her show.

He accepted. And because he added so much value, as a precession effect he got invited back a second time. When he went back a second time, he added so much value that eventually Oprah asked Dr. Phil if he would like his own segment. Dr. Phil then added so much value on his own segment, she asked if he would like his own show. Since that time Dr. Phil has sold millions of copies of his book. He's now known all over the world through his television program and has become a huge business success.

Dr. Phil created his success as a byproduct of adding value. I have built my company on this exact principle. When I started my company at the age of twenty-eight back in 1999, I was very green in terms of business skills. But I had an ability, and the ability was to help people make more sales. By me focusing on helping people make more sales, my business kept on growing and growing and growing. Over time, I started to get better and better at business.

During your sales process and sales presentation, focus on the customer and on adding value, regardless of how well or how poorly you are doing. When we struggle in sales, we tend to become desperate for the sale. I want to challenge you that, if you are ever at a point where you are struggling, leave your troubles outside of the sales presentation, whether you are delivering it over the phone or face-to-face. **Go into that sales presentation and focus 100 percent on adding value to the client.** As a result, you will be influencing at the highest level, and thus be far more likely to make the sale and start earning the commissions that you need in order to get yourself out of your negative financial situation. You also will generate a great deal of repeat and referral business.

Precession in Action

One of my star clients is Debbie Severn. When I met Debbie, who is in financial services, a number of years ago, she had a huge resistance to selling. This is very common not just in financial services, but in many sales industries. I taught Debbie that selling equals service, and to sell from a place of honesty, integrity, and compassion. I also taught her the precession effect. I told her, "Debbie, when you go and meet with your client, forget about your commission. Focus 100 percent of your attention on adding value to your client. The commissions will take care of themselves."

Several months later during a conference call with an advanced training group, I asked if anyone had a victory they'd like to share. Debbie said she did. She said, "Eric, I got my first million dollar client."

I said, "Debbie, congratulations on selling your first million dollar life insurance policy."

She said, "That's not what I said."

Now, I heard that she sold her first million dollar life insurance policy. Remember me saying we hear what we want to hear?

I said, "Debbie, what did you say?"

"I got my first million dollar client."

"What does that mean?"

"It means that a client invested over a million dollars with me!"

"Oh, that's obviously a little different than selling a million dollar life insurance policy," I enthused. "Debbie, how did you do it?"

"Well, the husband of one of my clients unfortunately passed, and she got a large life insurance settlement. And she was looking for somebody that she trusted to help her manage the money. And because of who I was—being in the sales presentation and focusing on adding value—she said that she was comfortable in having me oversee the money."

Another quick story about precession features my star client, Scott Taylor. Scott attended one of my seminars, then signed up to do advanced training with me. I asked Scott, "What's one comfort zone that you're willing to expand between now and when we meet again in ninety days?"

He said, "Public speaking."

"Great!" I replied. "How many speeches are you willing to give between now and when I see you at our next session?"

"One."

"You said 'four,' right?" I teased him.

He laughed and said, okay, four.

Well, Scott went and did those four. And now he's done over thirty front-of-room speeches. When I met Scott, he had a fear of public speaking, yet he has had a desire to speak since the early 1980s. So, for more than twenty years, Scott had the dream to be a speaker, and I helped him break through that.

Recently Scott sent me an email. One of Scott's success stories was featured in "spiritual entrepreneur" John Assaraf's book *The Answer*. John is an amazing person. He was featured in *The Secret*, a movie about optimist thinking. Donny Deutsch asked John to be on his show called *The Big Idea*. Donny asked John to bring some of his successful clients with him. Scott got a call from one of the producers for *The Big Idea* to appear on the show with John Assaraf. Here is what Scott told me after he appeared on the show:

> *"Eric, if I had never received your help and broken through my fear of public speaking, when I was asked up here on this television program I probably would have declined the invitation, stating that I couldn't make it. Thank you for all that you have done for me."*

Exercise

Can you remember a time when the "precession principle" happened to you, i.e., something positive that came from something else? What happened?

_____

_____

_____

_____

Now think about a situation in your life right now—ideally a sales-related situation—where you've been too focused on "you" and not on adding value to the customer. How has this situation gone to date?

_____

_____

_____

_____

What can you do to "right the ship," i.e., to focus on adding value rather than on your goals or desires?

_____

_____

_____

_____

Ideas Into Action

When Scott attended his first seminar with me, he didn't know I was going to help him overcome his fear of public speaking. He attended a _sales_ seminar. It had nothing to do with public speaking. He didn't know that eventually he would be on Donny Deutsch's show.

Here is a funny story about how Scott and I met. A number of years ago I ruptured my Achilles tendon. I had to have surgery to fix it and I was in a cast for several months. I was scheduled to teach a seminar called The Close in San Diego while I was still in my cast. A client called me and hired me to do a week of consulting in LA the week before The Close seminar. I did the week of consulting and now I needed to get down to San Diego to teach the seminar.

I had one problem: because I was in a cast I needed a ride to San Diego because I couldn't drive. Scott lives in LA. I saw he was registered to attend the event. The Close seminar was a free seminar this time. Scott signed up for the seminar but knew very little about me. We had never met in person before. I called Scott and got his voice mail. "Scott, this is Eric Lofholm," I said. "You are scheduled to come to my seminar in San Diego this weekend. I am in LA and I am looking for a ride to San Diego. Can you give me a ride? Call me back at (916) 626-6820." I didn't tell Scott that I needed the ride because I was in a cast and couldn't drive.

When Scott got the message he probably thought, *Who is this nut calling me and asking me for a ride to his seminar?* Scott didn't call me back and he reluctantly and skeptically went to the seminar. Little did he know his life was going to change. Isn't that a funny story? As I type this I am cracking up. (As I am writing this section I am at the Kona Kia Hotel in San Diego at Shelter Island. It is a beautiful day—sunny and about 70 degrees. I am listening to Bob Marley and following the San Francisco Giants on ESPN.com. This is the life!)

The universe rewards people who take action differently than those who don't.

Key Points Review

- The universe rewards people who take action differently than those who don't.

- Precession—the unexpected and almost always positive side effect when you take action.

- Greatness in sales comes by focusing on adding value to the customer.

PART II

The Outer Game
of Selling

In Part Two, I'm going to share with you my Process of Influence. Selling has a step-by-step process, very similar to having a meal at a restaurant like Olive Garden. If you and I went to Olive Garden, the greeter would ask, "How many in your party?" Then we would be seated at a table, and our server would ask if wanted drinks, appetizers, an entrée, and, later, dessert. When we were finished eating, the server would bring the bill—along with some green Andes Mints, an Olive Garden tradition.

At Olive Garden, do they ever come over before you have been seated and ask, "Would you like to start off with a slice of cheesecake?" No, that's not the process. Selling has its own process. It's simple and very effective. Unfortunately, most people in the world don't know the process. When you know the process and then ultimately master it, selling becomes simple, easy, fun, and most of all, very effective.

I call my sales process the Sales Mountain. At the base of the mountain, we begin with lead generation, then appointment setting, then a live presentation (either face to face or via phone). First we establish trust and building rapport. Next, you identify customer needs, share benefits, close, handle objections, then close again if the prospect has objections. If we don't close the sale and the prospect is still interested, we then follow up.

Once you master the sales process you will become more effective with every presentation you deliver.

The Sales Mountain

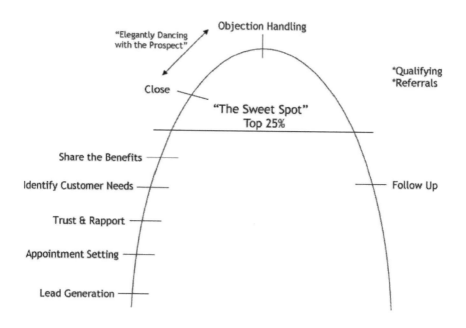

Chapter 3

The Process
of Influence

To illustrate the process of influence and how it fits into what we've already covered, imagine seeing yourself in the role of a telemarketer. For me this is easy, because my first sales job was selling over the phone. If you've never had a telemarketing job, you've probably still received many sales calls in your life. Imagine being the person making that call. What's the process you have to go through?

First of all, you've got to get yourself mentally and emotionally prepared to make cold calls to total strangers, most of whom will reject what you're offering. This takes motivation, determination, courage, and perseverance. That's where having the right mindset is crucial. That's what we covered in Part I.

But just being brave and determined enough to make cold calls isn't enough to be a telemarketer. For one thing, you also need to have a list of people to call.

You need to know what you're going to do when they pick up the phone. What are you trying to accomplish? Are you trying to persuade them to let your representative visit them for a sales appointment? Are you trying to get their permission to mail them some sales literature? Are you trying to get them to buy something over the phone? What action do you want to result from the call?

Finally, what are you going to say to achieve the results you want? What is your sales script? How will you say hello? What language will you use to explain why you're calling? What will you say to persuade your caller to continue listening to you instead of hanging up?

These are some of the things that factor into whether a telemarketing call results in a quick disconnection or a sales appointment. These are some of the steps in the process of influence.

The general steps are the same whether you're selling over the phone, face to face, or over the Internet. Getting the right mindset was the first step, and we covered it in Part I. Now let's talk about the next steps.

From Inner Game to Outer Game

I mentioned earlier that the structure of this book is based on the three top ways you can elevate your sales results:

Part I: Inner Game

Part II: Outer Game

Part III: Action

The inner game is the mental side of selling that we covered in Part I. It is your beliefs, your comfort zone, how you deal with rejection. It's the telemarketer getting psyched up to start making their daily quota of cold calls. It's the sales representative preparing for a big sales meeting. It's the consultant getting ready to meet that big client they've been trying to land.

Here in Part II we're shifting our focus to the outer game. The outer game is the tactical side of selling: what you say, when you say it, how you say it. Then in Part III we'll move on to taking action.

The outer game includes:

Three key systems for growing any business

Eight steps to making a sale

In the rest of this chapter I'll give you an overview of these. The following chapters will go into more detail on each item.

The Three Key Business Systems

Pay close attention here, because what I'm about to tell you is *one of the biggest ideas in this book*. In any industry, there are three keys to growing any business:

1. Lead generation
2. Appointment setting
3. Lead conversion

These three systems follow a logical sequence:

- *Lead generation* is making contact with people who want to buy from you
- *Appointment setting* is creating opportunities to deliver sales presentations to people who want to buy from you
- *Lead conversion* is delivering sales presentations

For each of these systems, you can improve your results by applying the three ways to elevate your results: inner game, outer game, and action. *The whole secret to improving your sales outer game is applying this central idea.* Grasp this principle and you grasp the essence of this book. Start applying this principle and you are on your way to becoming a sales master.

The Eight Steps in Making a Sale: Sales Mountain

As you can see from looking at the sequence of the three key business systems, the bottom line is lead conversion: that's where you close sales and make money. If we break down the process of lead conversion and include lead generation and appointment setting, we can divide the process of making a sale into eight steps. To help my students visualize and memorize these eight steps, I call them "climbing Sales Mountain." Here are the eight steps in Sales Mountain:

1. Lead generation
2. Appointment setting
3. Building trust and rapport

4. Identifying customer needs

5. Sharing benefits

6. Closing

7. Objection handling

8. Following up

If you look at the Sales Mountain diagram, you will also notice there are two "extra" steps with asterisks next to them, bringing the total from eight to ten steps:

- Qualifying
- Referrals

These last two items have asterisks because they are "wild cards" with special properties that can affect their inclusion and order in the sequence. With respect to qualifying, not all products and services require qualifying. For instance, if I'm inviting people to a free seminar, everyone is welcome, there's no need to qualify. On the other hand, if I'm selling a $10,000 coaching program I need to qualify the person to avoid wasting both of our time.

With respect to referrals, referrals can be incorporated into any step in the sales process, making their place in the sequence flexible. This is why referrals is also a wild card.

We'll come back to the topics of qualifying and referrals in later chapters. For now just notice that in addition to the eight main steps, there are two "extra" steps in Sales Mountain. In the chapters that follow we'll go deeper into the details of each step.

Staying in the Conversation

Among all the distinctions that I have to share with you, the most important and powerful one—not only as it relates to you becoming a master persuader and a master influencer—is a concept that I call *stay in the conversation*.

Let me share with you an example of what "stay in the conversation" isn't.

Many years ago, Jarris and I attended a Gary Smalley seminar. Gary Smalley is one of the top relationship experts in the world. We went to the seminar that night and Gary is a wonderful speaker. He shared some great ideas. In fact, he shared an idea of how to transform your communication with your spouse or significant other—something very helpful if you've had one of those times in your relationship where you're fighting and all of the communication has broken down. For me, it would be one of those nights where I would be expecting to sleep on the couch. And Gary shared an idea that night on how to transform the communication and break through a heated argument. And the technique was phenomenal. And I can share with you, my wife and I have used the technique personally several times, and it has actually worked.

Would you like me to share that technique with you? I have hidden the technique later in this book and if you would like to learn it, read thoroughly and you'll discover it.

Gary Smalley's seminar that night was great—he is an amazing presenter, he had some phenomenal ideas. Regrettably, I didn't stay in the conversation with Gary. I haven't been to one of his seminars since, even though he was great at what he does, and I highly recommend him.

Now, on the other hand, I met Dr. Moine about twenty years ago. And I have continued to stay in the conversation with Dr Moine and I will always do so, until one of us is no longer alive. That's how important this distinction is. In fact, it is the number one distinction that I teach. If I ever ask you, "What is the number one distinction that I teach?" the answer is "stay in the conversation."

Reading this book is one of the multiple ways I've designed to help you stay in the conversation with me on an ongoing basis, just like I'm staying in the conversation with Dr. Moine, so I can develop you as a sales champion just like he's developed me. In addition to this book, another way you can stay in the conversation is through my Protégé programs. A third way is through my audio products. Another way is through my DVDs. Yet another is through the Eric Lofholm Sales System, or through my Sales Script Writing Club or my Inner Circle. You could also choose to work with one of my coaches. These are all structures designed to help you achieve your best.

I was introduced to the idea of "stay in the conversation" by Loral Langemeier. I went through Loral's one-year wealth-building program.

Here's one of the points that Loral makes: When most couples talk about money, do they have a positive or negative conversation about money? That's right: a negative conversation!

In order to create wealth, what kind of conversation do you need to have? A positive conversation or a negative conversation? Of course, the answer is a positive conversation about wealth building.

So Loral created a company that creates a space for people like you and me to be in a positive conversation about wealth building. When I went through her program, she called it "staying in the conversation" as it related to wealth building. This was a positive conversation about wealth building. Her website is **www.liveoutloud.com**.

Remember, I look at life through the sales lens. I immediately thought of how I could use the "stay in the conversation" concept with my company.

In order for you to become a master influencer, you must get into a positive conversation about sales. By reading this book you are having a conversation with me about sales and business excellence. I invite you to "stay in the conversation" with me. One of the things I've learned is simply this: You can only get so far on your own. The level of persuasion and influence that I've had the opportunity to achieve—I didn't get here by myself. Many mentors and coaches helped lift me up to that higher level of success. I want you to know that my company is here to support you in a variety of ways and help lift you up to that next level of success.

To help you reach the next level of success, I and my staff of trainers offer additional training support to help you master the material taught in this book. My affordably-priced Silver Protégé program (also called the Unstoppable Selling System) includes additional training materials in PDF, audio, and video format, plus weekly group coaching calls led by me personally. You can ask me questions directly, and you also get one of my certified sales trainers assigned to help you. You even get an opportunity to get certified by me yourself after passing a test on the exact same material you'll be learning in this book. If you want to get a free taste of what my training program is like, go to my website to sign up for my free 21-video series on how to close:

http://www.saleschampion.com

I encourage you to check out my videos so you can see the value of continuing in the conversation with me and letting me help you master the material in this book.

Ideas into Action

To put the ideas in this chapter into action, I'd like to suggest you take three main actions:

First, commit to memorizing the key distinctions laid out in this chapter and taught in more detail in the rest of this book:

- The three main ways you can elevate your sales results: Inner Game vs. Outer Game vs. Action
- The three key business systems: lead generation, appointment setting, and lead conversion
- The eight steps in Sales Mountain (plus the two "extra steps")

Second, commit to staying in the conversation so you can continue to learn from me and letting me help you master this material.

Third, to help you stay in the conversation, visit my website and watch my free videos, and if you find what I teach helpful, consider signing up for more of my training and getting certified in my sales system:

http://www.saleschampion.com

Key Points Review

- Influence is a process.
- The three main ways you can elevate your sales results are by improving your Inner Game, your Outer Game, and your Action.
- The three business systems that impact sales are lead generation, appointment setting, and lead conversion.
- The process of making a sale is symbolized by the image of climbing Sales Mountain, which has eight main steps (lead generation, appointment setting, building trust and rapport, identifying customer needs, sharing benefits, closing, objection handling, and following up) and two "extra" steps that can arise anywhere in the sequence (qualifying and referrals).
- The most important distinction is *staying in the conversation*.
- You can stay in the conversation by checking out my free video training and learning more about my training programs by visiting my website:

http://www.saleschampion.com

Chapter 4

Generating
Unlimited Leads

I've mentioned how I've broken *The System* into three key sections, as ways to elevate your sales results: the Inner Game, the Outer Game and Action. Well, there are three ways for you to generate more leads: the Inner Game of Lead Generation, the Outer Game of Lead Generation, and Action.

The Inner Game of Lead Generation revolves around your mindset, or belief, about leads. The Outer Game of Lead Generation focuses on actual tactics of lead generation—such as the strategies and systems you use to generate leads. Finally, you must take action by doing what you know you need to be doing to generate leads.

The Inner Game of Lead Generation

The purpose of generating a lead is to generate a lead. Simple, right? When I share this statement in seminars, I usually get a chuckle from the audience. Yet this is one of the most profound distinctions that I have ever discovered about selling. What it allows you to do is **look at lead generation as a stand-alone activity in the sales process.** In other words, if you attended a networking event and met someone you were interested in doing business with, the only thing that you need to do is simply get their contact information. That's all.

One of the biggest mistakes I see people in the influence process make is to try to accomplish too much too soon. Instead of focusing solely on generating the lead, they begin delivering their sales presentation at the networking event. Now, I am using a networking event as a metaphor. It's really any way that you meet the prospect—whether you meet them online or offline, whether you meet them face to face or over the phone. Energy either attracts or it repels. If you go beyond just lead generation in the initial contact with the prospect, chances are you are going to try and do too much too soon. This creates a repelling energy.

This gets back to your lead generation mindset. Imagine a circle. This circle represents all of the opportunities available for you. Pretend that you took a pencil and made a dot in the center of that circle. That dot represents all of the business that you are capable of doing; anything more than that dot, and your cup would be overflowing. Talk about an abundant mindset, right? Right! Develop this mindset that there are more leads out there than what you could possibly service in your target market. This also takes the pressure off of you to turn every lead into business.

Here's another great mindset: "I have an easy time generating leads. I am a lead generating magnet. I am a lead generation master." Imagine if you repeated these three sentences once in the morning and once at night before going to bed for thirty days.

I also strongly suggest to my clients to develop a lead generating goal. Goals act like magnets—when you set a goal, you will attract the key elements needed to accomplish that goal. Your goal should be to develop a set number of new leads to be added to your database within a set period of time. Here's an example:

My goal is to develop 25 new leads in the month of October.

Your goal might be daily, weekly, or monthly. You might have a series of goals for different time periods. Whatever the case, be sure to:

1. Write down your goals.
2. Refer to these on a regular basis.
3. Measure, track, and review your results.

Please note that I just used a key term for lead generation: database. Once you have a lead, whether it's a business card, their contact information, or a referral, what I want you to do with that lead is put the lead in your database. A database is simply a sales productivity tool that keeps all of your leads organized.

In my database, I have my main database, which contains every single contact I have ever entered, along with information about that lead, such as the prospect or client's name, email address, phone number, different products that they have purchased from me, where they are at in the sales cycle, and so on. My database keeps track of all of that. Most databases also can be segmented into subgroups. For example, I have my entire database, and I also have a subgroup within my entire database of everyone in my Protégé program. A database is a critical aspect of your business.

Right now, I am assuming that you know what a database is, and that you have and use one. If, in your case, either of these assumptions isn't true, make it a point to go online and learn about databases.

The Outer Game of Lead Generation: Ideas + Action = Results

Now that you've developed the proper mindset regarding lead generation, let's get into specific ways to land more leads.

Tool 1: Ask

Let's begin with a mind-blower: How about asking for a lead? When I meet someone, one of my favorite lead generation strategies is simply to say, "Would you like to exchange business cards?" It works almost every single time.

If the prospect doesn't have a business card, then I'll simply say, "Can I get your contact information? I would love to stay in touch with you." They can then jot their information down on a piece of paper and give to me.

Key Point

Many people leave the back of their business card blank, both to write notes when giving their card to other people, or to jot down and then save information provided by others. Many marketing folks I know strongly advocate that you print key information about your company on the back of your business card—this becomes, in effect, a mini-ad for your company.

Both have their benefits and drawbacks. If you do print on the back of your business card, be ready to acquire contact information from those who don't have a business card at the time you meet them.

Tool 2: Use the Fish bowl

When I train network marketers, I teach them to get a list of 200 people that they can contact to introduce their business opportunity to. At first, they sometimes go, "Eric, how am I possibly going to get 200 leads?" I say, "Don't worry about it. Simply set the goal and watch what happens."

One time I taught this strategy to a gentleman in a company called World Financial Group. He reported back to me that he went to a Chamber of Commerce meeting. At the meeting, they held a raffle. How did people enter? By dropping in their business card in a fish bowl. They pulled one business card out, and that person won the prize. The person I had trained didn't care about the prize; he had his eye on that fish bowl. What was the person doing the raffle going to do with those business cards? At the end of the meeting he watched the person in charge of the fish bowl go over to the garbage can. He was about to dump the business cards in the garbage can and my smart trainee said, "Whoa, whoa, whoa, what are you going to do with those business cards?"

The person said, "I'm going to throw them away. Why? Did you want them?"

"Sure!" my trainee replied.

There were sixty-seven business cards. These were all people in his target market. He put those leads in his database. He then could now call those prospects up and say, "My name is so-and-so, I got your card at the Chamber of Commerce meeting that you recently attended. I was there as well," and he could use that as the lead-in. The next time you're at an event with a raffle, forget about winning a small gift—look for the big gift, the cards inside the fishbowl!

Tool 3: Follow Your Money

"Follow Your Money" doesn't work in every industry, but it works in many. Review this strategy to see if it might work for you.

When you pay someone money, you become their customer. You have a unique relationship with them; because you pay them money, there's an implied rapport. So think about all of the people who you pay money to: where you get your car fixed, where you get your hair done, where you get your nails done, your doctor, your chiropractor, the manager of the grocery store that you go to, the owner of your favorite restaurant, and so on. Think of all of the places where you spend money and ask yourself the question: Are those people in my target market?

If you're a real estate agent, they are. If you're a loan officer, they are. If you are in network marketing, they are. If you sell insurance, they probably are. And if that's true, I want to suggest that you put every single person that you pay money to into your database and start marketing to those folks.

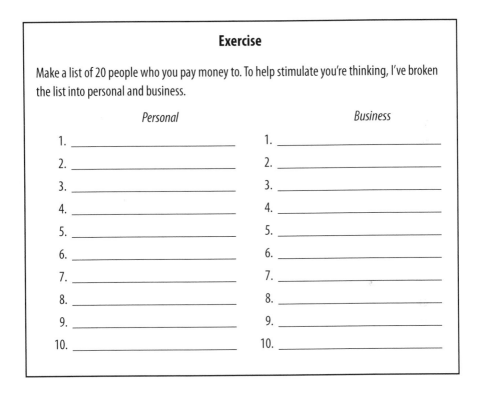

Exercise

Make a list of 20 people who you pay money to. To help stimulate you're thinking, I've broken the list into personal and business.

Personal	*Business*
1. _____	1. _____
2. _____	2. _____
3. _____	3. _____
4. _____	4. _____
5. _____	5. _____
6. _____	6. _____
7. _____	7. _____
8. _____	8. _____
9. _____	9. _____
10. _____	10. _____

Here's how to use this strategy at a restaurant. The next time you go to that favorite restaurant, ask the server to bring over the owner. When the owner comes to the table, introduce yourself and use a little flattery—tell the owner that it's one of your favorite eateries and that you absolutely love to dine there. At the end of your conversation, let the owner know that you are a real estate agent and that if they ever have a need for anything related to real estate to let you know. That's all you say.

Immediately put the owner as a lead in your database. Now you can begin marketing to that person. The next time you go to the restaurant two or three weeks later, make sure you say "hi" to the owner. Again, resist the urge to prospect at that point. Simply build rapport. Over time, you'll be amazed at how many of these contacts turn into business.

Tool 4: Referrals

You can generate leads with *referrals*, or people's names given to you by someone you know or are in contact with.

When it comes to referrals, you want to have a referral system. I used a very basic, but very effective one, when I was a trainer for the Tony Robbins organization. I would do front-of-the-room presentations inside of companies to promote Tony's one-day business seminar called The Competitive Edge. Near the end of my presentation, I would hand out a half sheet of paper that had a place for the prospect/participant to write down their name and up to five referrals. Not only did I let the audience know what a good referral was for me, I told them that if you gave me three or more referrals, I would give them a Tony Robbins audio cassette. I averaged ten referrals per appointment. I have used that strategy for over ten years now. I used it when I worked for Tony Robbins and now I use it with my own company. That one idea has generated over ten thousand referrals. Now *that* is a referral system!

One of my star clients, Doak Belt, is in financial services, and I am a client of his. Doak, who has a very interesting referral system, called me one day and said, "Eric, I am growing my business right now with referrals, and it would really mean a lot to me if you'd help me with some referrals. What I'd like to do is schedule a time where we can spend ten or fifteen minutes on the phone when you are in front of your database on your computer. Would you be willing to help me out?" He then set a referral appointment with me.

When Doak called for our phone meeting, he began by educating me on what a good referral was for him. "Eric," he said, "I am looking for small business owners that are homeowners and who are married with children. I also want to work with people who you think would be fun for me to work with."

I gave Doak three names. After I gave him each name, he said, "Eric, do you have the mailing address of this referral?"

I was a little confused. "Doak, I've never had someone ask me for a mailing address when asking for a referral. Why do you want their mailing address?"

"Well, once I have their contact and their mailing address, I put them in my database," Doak replied. "Then I send the referral a letter prior to calling them, letting the referral know that, in your case, 'Eric referred you to me,' and to be expecting my phone call."

"Doak, that's great. Why do you do that?"

"Well, in half the cases, the person that was the referral will call you up and say, 'I got this letter from this guy Doak, is he the real deal?'"

I later learned that two of the three referrals I gave Doak that day became his clients. Since then, Doak has scheduled three other referral appointments with me.

The idea behind a system is that you do it over and over and over again. So when you are thinking about leads, think in terms of a Lead Generation System.

Tool 5: The POI Strategy

Here's my favorite lead generation idea—what I call the POI strategy. POI stands for "Person(s) Of Influence." To visualize the POI concept, picture the letters "POI" with a triangle beneath them. The triangle beneath the POI is the POI's network.

Everyone in the world has a network, but not everyone is a POI. A POI is someone who has *your target market* in their network. To make this strategy work, go to the POI and influence the Person Of Influence to endorse you, promote you, edify you, refer you, or give you access to their network. This will give you hot fresh leads of people ready to buy from you now . . . and in many cases, you receive these leads at zero cost to you.

As a sales trainer, I identify POIs, build relationships with those POIs, then influence them to give me access to their network. I do this with large sales organizations. I do this with network marketing companies. I do this with other speakers and trainers with large email lists. I do this with associations.

The key to making this work is this: *I* approach *them*. When you want to build a relationship with a POI, you're going to influence them in a very similar way that you would influence anyone. You want to enter their world, find out what is important to them. Obviously when you build a relationship with a POI, we know what's in it for you—you gain access to their network. But what benefits can you provide to the POI?

Let me give you a specific example of how I structure relationships like this. It's called a Reciprocal Referral Relationship. Let me explain. I'll identify a POI who has my target market in their network. For example, D.C. Cordova, owner of Excellerated Business Schools, does not do sales training—she provides business performance training for entrepreneurs, business owners, commission sales people, and network marketers. She has a wonderful program that I have personally attended and believe in. So I regularly promote D.C.'s company and seminars to my network. In return, D.C. believes in my work, so she regularly promotes me to her network of people. This is called a Reciprocal Referral Relationship.

I said earlier that goals act like magnets. What if you set a goal to create ten Reciprocal Referral Relationships? If you are real estate agent, you'd create that kind of relationship with someone who sells insurance, someone who sells cars, someone who does tax preparation, someone who does printing, and so forth. Ask yourself this question:

Who has my customers inside their database?

Set an intention to create a relationship with ten POIs. I guarantee your sales will double within a set period of time.

Tool 6: Climb the Ladder Selling

Let me give you two nuances to the POI concept. I call the first "Climb The Ladder Selling." Here, you don't know the POI, but you know somebody who does. For example, maybe you're selling to a company and know one of the employees, but you don't know the CEO. To utilize "Climb the Ladder Selling," you would approach the employee and ask for an introduction to the CEO.

Tool 7: The House List

Your house list is your list of prospects, customers, and clients. A buyer is a buyer is a buyer. With this in mind, systematically review your house lists (i.e., database) and offer these contacts additional products and services.

Let me give you example. You have purchased this book (or have been given it as a gift). That's great—I've supplied you value (lot's of it!), and you in turn have paid me a fee. But I don't want our relationship to end here; I have an intention to become your sales training solution for life. Now, that doesn't mean that you won't have other mentors in training success and sales. It means that my intention is to be one of those people in your life you tap for expertise and ideas, and for that relationship to be lifelong.

To support that intention, I have multiple products and services to help develop you into a sales champion: coaching programs, seminars, boot camps, advanced training, audio CDs, DVDs, conference calls, and so on. I let my house list know about these products all the time.

I want to encourage you now to create an intention to become your clients' solution for life. One of my clients, Beth Conway, is a real estate agent in Rocklin, California, where I live. I taught her this concept. It's Beth's intention to become my real estate solution for life.

This can apply to virtually any field. I have bought about probably ten cars through the years, almost all at car dealerships. I've never once had someone sell me a car and create an intention to be my car solution for life. This one idea could transform your sales results forever—to become someone's (insert your product or service) solution for life.

Tool 8: Squeeze Page

A squeeze page is one-page website where you offer something of value (such as information) for free, in exchange for receiving the prospect's contact information. An example of a squeeze page is **freesalesscriptingreport.com**. When you go to that website, you can request a report on sales scripting at no charge. The form you fill out there is connected to my database. In other words, the prospect is entering their information directly into my database. My database then puts that prospect into the group—free sales scripting report—within my main database (which they also are part of). My database then auto-responds the promised report to the prospect. I now have a lead. Even better, I know that this lead is someone who is interested in sales scripting. I can then systematically contact this person over time, offering them sales training services and sales scripting services.

To create your own squeeze page, think about what information your prospect would want prior to making a buying decision. If you are a listing agent for real estate, consider a free report, such as *Seven Ways to Sell Your Home for Maximum Profit*.

Folks, this is powerful. I know there will be one reader who reads this section of the book, then takes this one idea, creates a squeeze page, and generates over ten thousand leads at virtually zero cost, bringing in several million dollars in additional sales. Will you be the one?

Tool 9: Recycling Leads

I also advocate recycling leads—calling a lead every ninety days until they say "yes" to your offer. Now I am not saying you *should* call them every ninety days; I am saying that you *can* call them up to every ninety days and offer them the exact same offer (or offer something different).

Tool 10: Public Speaking

I built my business via public speaking. I started my business in San Diego, California. I gave speeches to any group within a ninety-mile radius of my home: sales teams, network-marketing teams, Chambers of Commerce, network meetings, and so forth. I would typically give one speech per day. For each speech, I would be in front of an average of ten people. After providing something of value (i.e., information), I would then offer my sales training services. I generated thousands and thousands of leads—and hundreds of thousands of dollars worth of business—utilizing this strategy.

Later on, I was introduced to the idea of conference calls. At first I thought, "No one is going to buy my sales training services on conference calls. I have to give the presentation face to face." But I tried it out, and sure enough, people just as easily bought on conference calls as they did selling face-to-face, front-of-the-room. When I did conference calls, I would have people register for the call on a special landing page on my website. When somebody registered for the call, I now had a lead I could market to for life *whether they attended the call or not.*

There are many ways to leverage your speeches or conference calls. For example, you could record the conference call and put the recording on an audio CD, or make it available on a website as an audio download. You can also transcribe the conference call or speech and make that available.

One more powerful conference call idea is to go to someone else who has a large email list, and ask them to promote your conference call or squeeze page to their email l. Michael Senoff of **hardtofindseminars.com** has a large email list. Michael enjoys my sales training content. He recently interviewed me, then made the interview available to his database. Twenty-four hours after he emailed his database, more than 300 people had opted in on my website, which created 300 brand new leads for me to offer additional sales training products and services to, at zero cost.

(The interview I did with Michael was fantastic. In fact, it was the best interview I have ever done because Michael is an amazing interviewer. He also transcribed the interview. If you would like a copy of that audio and the transcription, please visit **makingmoresales.com/michael.htm**.)

Ideas Into Action

This chapter was filled with awesome ideas to help you generate unlimited leads. I want to strongly encourage you to read this chapter seven times, take the best ideas based on your business and personal situation, and immediately implement those ideas.

Key Points Review

- Lead generation requires a proper mindset.

- You must believe in abundance when it comes to lead generation.

- Set, track, and review lead generation goals.

- Use a lead generation/sales database.

- There are many lead generation tools and ideas—review the eleven presented in this chapter seven times, select the ones that will work best for you, and implement.

Chapter 5

Setting Unlimited Appointments

I hope you consider *appointment setting* as a critical skill set for a successful sales career, because it is. Appointments are the catalyst that skyrockets your sales results. The three ways to increase your appointment setting results include the Inner Game, the Outer Game, and Action.

As I stated in previous chapters, the Inner Game of appointment setting is your mindset about appointment setting—it's your comfort zones around appointment setting. The Outer Game focuses on the tactical side of setting appointments—what you say, when you say it, how you say it, and so on. It's your follow-up system; it's how you keep your leads organized; it's your database. The third component is action. Here you must will yourself to follow through and take action by doing what you know you should be doing to set successful appointments.

Develop the Proper Mindset

Let's begin by talking about the "appointment setting" mindset. I strongly suggest you adopting the following mindsets:

1. There are more potential appointments than what you can logistically attend.

2. There are too many leads—you can't possible help everyone.

3. Appointment setting is fun and easy.

Avoid saying:

1. Appointment setting is hard.

2. I am not good at appointment setting.

3. I am not good at sales.

Your appointment setting will become stronger when you focus on the *value* that you can provide a new client. When it comes to appointment setting, prospects' minds act like a teeter-totter: on one side is time; on the other, value. When a prospect tells you, "I don't have the time to meet with you," that's not true. We always find the time to do important things. What they are really saying is that you haven't built enough value in the appointment yet.

Remember, too, that appointment setting isn't about closing the sale. In other words, don't make it too complicated. Your desired outcome should be to set the appointment—not to sell your product or service. Again, here's a key point: *The benefits of the appointment are different than the benefits of your product or service.* To build value in your appointment, clearly communicate the stand-alone benefits that the prospect is going to receive by agreeing to meet with you.

The timeshare industry has mastered this value concept. If you have ever gone to a resort town like Cancun, Mexico or Honolulu, Hawaii, chances are you have been approached by somebody offering to give you money or some type of vacation incentive if you will sit through a timeshare presentation. When I was in Cancun, someone asked, "Are there any activities that you and your wife would like to do?" I told the person, "Well, I'm interested in going on the lobster cruise." They said, "How would you like to go lobster cruise for free?"

My mind went *ka-ching*! I knew the lobster cruise cost $60 per person. When I asked how that would work, they said, "All you need to do is sit through a ninety-minute presentation. You don't have to buy anything. At the end of the presentation I will give you two tickets to the lobster cruise." So, the benefit, or value, of that timeshare presentation was two tickets to the lobster cruise.

Consider this example of a real estate agent and think about how this relates to what you sell. A real estate agent attempting to secure a listing appointment could communicate the following stand-alone benefits of the appointment.

"When we meet, it will be at a time that is convenient for you."

"I'll deliver a market analysis and share with you what all the properties like yours have sold for in the area."

"I'll share with you my vision on how I would market your property. I'll answer all your questions. Then at the end of the appointment you will have the opportunity to hire me as your real estate agent if you feel comfortable, and if not, then no problem. Sound good?"

Now the beauty of what I just shared is that this appointment has been "framed" as an opportunity for the prospect to hire you. Why is this important? Oftentimes a prospect won't meet with you because they are afraid that you are going to use high-pressure sales techniques to close the sale. (This is called a non-stated objection; they don't tell you that's why they are unwilling to meet with you, but in many cases it's the real reason.)

However, when you say to the prospect, "… at the end of the meeting if you feel comfortable you will have the opportunity to hire me, and if not, then no problem, fair enough," you are communicating to the prospect that you "get it" and *won't* pressure them. In other words, you are letting them know that you are a professional.

A Track to Run On

Another great concept is called a "Track to Run On." I learned this from studying Ben Feldman, the world's greatest life insurance sales person. When Ben Feldman started in the insurance field his track to run on, or basic goal, was to sell three policies a week. As Ben became more successful, he continued to have a track to run on of signing three policies a week. As he continued to become even more successful, he still had the track to run on of three policies a week. And when he became the number one life insurance sales person in the world, he still had a track to run on of writing three policies a week. Even though he kept writing larger and larger policies and working with more and more successful clients, he kept his track to run on of three policies a week—because that goal was clear, simple, and easy to focus on.

When I was a salesperson for Tony Robbins in field presentations, my personal track to run on was one to two appointments set per day. Over the course of week, I would run ten and set five. Over the course of a month I would run forty and set twenty. I was able to set fewer appointments than what I ran because appointments would be supplemented by appointment setters that worked in Tony's corporate office. I focused every day on running two appointments and setting one; running ten a week and setting five; and I would book a week in advance.

As I'm writing this part of the book, it's Thursday. I can quickly look at my next week's calendar to see wether I have enough appointments on the calendar to run ten appointments. If the answer was "no," I would look for ways to generate more appointments, such as: What pending appointments do I have that I could call up and see if they would be willing to meet with me next week? What appointment do I have further out in the month that I could pull up to run even sooner? Who on my team might have some extra appointments that they might be willing to give me? What appointments have cancelled that I could call up and attempt to reschedule? Who can I call today to book an appointment for next week?

I would get these answers by following the principle of having a track to run on. Consider the following questions.

How much do you want to make this month? _____

How many appointments can you run in a month? _____

What is your track to run on? _____

Develop a Sales Plan

I can't stress enough how important it is to have a sales plan. Here's a formula to create a simple sales plan:

How much do you want to make this month? _____

How much revenue do you earn on average per run appointment?

_____

How many appointments do you need to run in order to achieve your financial goal? (Be sure to factor in your appointment cancellation percentage.) _____

Remember, your goal when setting an appointment is to set an appointment, not to sell a product or service. Setting appointments is the catalyst for a successful sales career. Imagine how your life would be different if you had as many appointments as you wanted.

Appointment Setting Strategies

Here are several appointment-setting ideas.

1. Reduce the risk

Reduce the risk means that when you ask for an appointment and the prospect says no, you ask for another appointment that provides less risk. Here's an example. My appointment setter called Wells Fargo in San Diego many years ago. She spoke with the vice president of sales, a woman named Martha Phillips. My appointment setter asked Martha if she would be willing to have me come out be a guest speaker to her branch managers to share some great ideas to increase sales, and also as an opportunity for me to introduce one of my sales training programs. Martha said that she was not interested. The appointment setter then applied "reduce the risk" and said to Martha, "How about we have Eric, the president of the company, come to your office and meet with you for only five minutes. After you meet with him, if you like what you hear you will have the opportunity to bring Eric in to one of your sales meetings, or one of your managers' meeting. And if not, then no problem. Fair enough?"

Martha said, fine, send him on out. So I went and met with Martha. She agreed to meet with me for five minutes. I came in and shared with her my background and how I felt that I could help her and her team. All of a sudden forty-five minutes had passed. I looked at my watch and I said, "Martha, I apologize. I have to run. I have another appointment that I need to get to." Needless to say, we had hit it off. Martha agreed to have me come out and speak. This turned in to a $10,000 consulting job, all by applying the principle "reduce the risk."

2. Set appointment setting goals

Goals remain critical success components, particularly when it comes to appointment setting. Be sure to set goals for your appointments for each day, week, and month. And be sure to review these daily.

3. Use preframing

Preframing simply means that you let the prospect know in advance what's going to happen. Here's a preframing example for someone selling financial services.

> *"Mr. Prospect, when I meet with you, in order for me to help you, I would like you to have your tax statements for the last two years ready to go. I'd also like you to have any insurance policies that you have and any financial statements for things like 401k's, saving accounts, stocks, etc. Can you have that ready for me when I meet with you?"* Almost every time they will agree. You have just preframed the prospect to have all that documentation ready.

4. Be ready for referrals

Appointment setting can be an excellent opportunity for referrals. For example, when talking to a company, you could ask if they have other offices in the area. If yes, simply ask, "Is there one person who, if they gave this the green light, could approve me to be a guest speaker in all the offices?" Note the person's name and contact info, and contact them to book the appointment.

5. Have a follow-up system

When the prospect says, "Call me back next Tuesday," have a system to keep your leads organized so you will successfully follow up with the client next Tuesday.

6. Follow up

Repeat this phrase every day: *Follow up, follow up, until they buy or die.* Remember, you are offering something of value. Take the appointment to a conclusion of a "yes" or a "no."

Appointment Tools & Techniques

I suggest you utilize these tools to aid in your appointment setting:

1. Have an appointment setting script.

2. Have a confirmation email.

3. Have an information email. We know the prospect is going ask you to send them some information so have an email response ready to go.

4. Create objection response scripts. These are powerful prepared responses when the prospect says, "I don't have the time." Or, "I need to think about it." Or, "Can you send me some information?" And so on.

5. Leads in your target market. You need an inventory of leads. If you're doing a telemarketing campaign, I suggest you have a minimum of 200 leads at all times.

6. Have a calendar.

7. Create blocked scheduled time. Think of this as an appointment you set with yourself—scheduled time to make your appointment-setting calls.

8. Track results. Track the number of appointments that you are setting on a daily, weekly, and monthly basis.

Use these appointment-setting techniques to help you secure more appointments:

1. Set appointments over the phone.

2. Set appointments with an email.

3. Book an appointment while at another appointment. Think about your dentist—before you leave, they make sure to schedule your next appointment even if it's six months out or longer.

4. Set an appointment at a seminar. I set appointments during breaks and before and after I am speaking.

5. Set automated appointment via a website.

6. Have others book your appointments. You could hire an appointment setter. Or you could create an internal referral, where someone within your organization (such as the accounting department) knows some-body who might benefit from your company's product or service, so they book the appointment for you.

Exercise

The ways to set appointments are almost limitless. What other ideas can you think of now?

_____

_____

_____

_____

Ideas Into Action

Appointment setting is a learned skill. In many cases it simply comes down to your intention to schedule as many appointments as you want. Make a decision today to apply these ideas and increase the number of appointments you are setting and running. Finally, consider this question: _What actions will you take immediately to improve your appointment setting skills?_

Key Points Review

- Appointment setting is critical to sales success.

- Great appointment setting requires the proper mindset, techniques, and tools.

- Don't try to sell your product or service—simply sell the appointment.

- To land more appointments, focus on the value you can provide prospects for attending the appointment.

- Develop appointment setting goals, track results, and review frequently.

Chapter 6

Building Instant Trust and Rapport

I consider trust and rapport the cornerstone of the sales process. Why? Simply because *people buy from people they like and trust.* When you consciously work on developing rapport and trust, you will make more sales.

Rapport is a state of harmony that we enter into with the prospect. Rapport focuses on harmony, oneness, and creating agreement. On a conscious level, we notice certain differences—things like he's taller than me, he's shorter, her hair is different than mine, she's younger than I am. On a subconscious level, however, we notice similarities. You want to bring those subconscious similarities to the surface using trust and rapport.

This can't be emphasized enough, especially because your prospect probably views you as a "salesperson," and in many cases that's a negative view. Rapport reduces resistance.

Rapport Foundation: Being Present

We each have our own model of the world; your model of the world is different from my model of the world. If you are married, you spouse's model of world is different from your model of the world. If you have a sales manager, your manager's model of the world is different from your model of the world. Your client's model of the world is different from our model of the world, and so on. To gain a deeper level of rapport, enter the world of your prospect and view their experience from their perspective. One of the Seven Habits from Stephen Covey's famous book *The Seven Habits of Highly Successful People* is first to understand, then be understood.

Let me give you an example. One time I was teaching a seminar in the San Francisco Bay Area. We went around the room and gave everyone an opportunity to share their name and a little bit about themselves. One woman shared that the night before she had gone to an Oakland Athletics baseball game. Now if you have a very limited amount of time to share and you're a woman and you share that you just went to an A's game, it's almost certain that you are a big Oakland A's baseball fan.

The next day at the seminar, during a section on trust and rapport, I said to this same woman, "Does the name Walt Weiss mean anything to you?" Her face lit up and she said, "Absolutely!" Now most of the people in the room had no clue what I was talking about. Walt Weiss was a short stop for the A's in the late 1980s. The fact that I knew the name Walt Weiss resonated with her—now we had something in common. And all of a sudden, we were like two peas in a pod. I had entered her world—in this case, her love of baseball, and particularly of the Oakland A's.

Here's another example of the power of rapport and trust. A number of years ago I was teaching a seminar, and I asked my friend Ben Gay III if he would come down to the seminar and do a training section for me. Ben is a legendary sale trainer; he has being training sales people for over forty years. He is the man behind *The Closers* book series. Ben agreed to do it as a favor. Ben came to the seminar and he told a story about doing some motivational speaking inside of San Quentin State Prison. At the time the notorious 1960s cult leader Charles Manson was at San Quentin and put out the word that he wanted a one-on-one meeting with Ben.

Now if you had the opportunity to be with Charles Manson one-on-one in his cell, would you take it? I know I wouldn't! But Ben, he's an adventurous type of person; he jumped at the opportunity to spend time with Manson. Ben shared this story with our group, and at the end of the training one of the participants in the room asked Ben what made Manson so persuasive. Ben shared some information that I have never forgotten. He said, "Well first let me share this with you. When you meet people that are highly persuasive, oftentimes they take a tremendous interest in you."

Ben talked about Bill Clinton, and he told the story of how one time the former President was talking to somebody and he was "being present" with that person. He was drinking a glass of water and as he drank the glass of water he maintained eye contact with this other person through the bottom of the glass of the water. When you spent time with Bill Clinton, you knew that you were important. Highly successful persuaders make you feel as if you are the most important person in the room.

Ben went on to add that when he spent time with Manson, he felt as though the convicted murder conspirator was being present with him and that Ben was the most important person in the room. Yes, he was the *only* person in the room, but Manson still created that feeling.

Now think about the opposite, when you are with someone yet they're not fully present—they're distracted, or otherwise preoccupied. We've all done this; I've done it! In fact, Ben's story hit me like a ton of bricks. I started thinking about all the times that my employees came to me, asking me questions, and I wasn't present with them. I was working on my computer and thus not fully present.

Think about this example: What do you do when you're talking to a prospect in the flesh and your cell phone rings? If you answer that cell phone, you're communicating to the prospect that they are not that important. One thing you can do to increase your level of trust and rapport is to stay present with your prospect. They will sense this and you will greatly enhance your trust and rapport.

Creating Rapport

Here are key ways to create rapport:

- Find common ground. Look for similarities between you and the prospect.
- Mirror and match your prospect's physiology. If they are sitting and cross their legs, you should cross your legs. Do they stand tall and look you in the eye? Stand tall and look them in the eye.

- Mirror and match your prospects speech rate and tonality. Do they speak loudly? You should as well.

- Mirror and match their language. Repeat phrases they use, use terms they use.

- Dress the way that your prospect would expect a professional in your industry to dress.

- Show the prospect that you have a solution to their problem.

- Do something nice for them.

- Treat others the way they would like to be treated. Treat others the way you would like to be treated.

- Be polite.

- Listen.

- Care about your client more than you care about your commission. To do this, put your energy on serving the client and adding value, and not on what you will get out of the transaction or interaction.

Exercise

For the next seven days, focus on ways of building rapport with everyone you meet or interact with, including friends, family members, even a waitress or your mailman. Try to determine which of the ways to build rapport just mentioned are particularly suited to you and your communication style.

Another extremely effective way to build trust and rapport is by being humorous. The performance hypnotist and salesman Marshall Sylver says, "Funny equals money." Humor builds rapport. Look for ways to incorporate humor into your presentation.

Remember my earlier story of, at my first real job, making over a hundred thousand...*hamburgers*? That's humor. In fact, I often show a picture of me in my McDonald's uniform, and in almost every case, people laugh. I've told that story over a thousand times, and it almost always produces the same result. That's a humor script designed to build a group rapport with the audience.

What are ways you can incorporate humor when you first meet a contact or prospect? Be sure to plan ahead; don't try to "wing it"—have your humor planned, just like I do with my speech about my first job at McDonald's.

Bonding

There's a level beyond trust and rapport called bonding. This is extremely important; in fact, what I'm about to share with you could help you create a sales breakthrough. The level beyond trust and rapport is to bond with your client. Bonding results when trust and rapport are present, and the relationship then moves to a stronger, mutually beneficial level. Let me give you a few examples.

The first one is about my friend and great trainer, Jill Lublin. Jill is a publicity expert. Last year, Jill had an accident, and both of her legs ended up in casts. One day I called her to say hello, and the person in her office explained that she wasn't available. I said, "This is her friend, Eric Lofholm, and I know she was in an accident and I want to see if there was anything I can do to help her. Do you know if there's anything that she needs?" The person said, kind of jokingly, "Well, as a matter of fact, there is something she needs. She needs a ride tomorrow from the LAX airport to where she's giving a speech".

I live in the Sacramento area in Northern California, which is hundreds of miles away from Southern California. So obviously I wasn't going to be able to give her a ride. Later, after I had hung up the phone, though, I started thinking about Jill's need. She needed a ride. I couldn't give her one myself. But how else could I make that happen?

Then it dawned on my—I have a friend who owns a limousine company in Southern California. I called my friend up, explained what I needed and that I'd return a similar favor to him one day, and he said sure. Jill got her ride. Even more importantly, my going the extra mile for her created a bond between us. Look for ways to do something similar with your clients.

KEY POINT

One interesting thing about trust and rapport is that once someone has purchased from you once, there's a certain level of rapport that is always present. This is an incredibly valuable distinction, because a buyer is a buyer is a buyer. One of the most common mistakes that salespeople make is to continue to look for the next sale from prospects, instead of deepening their relationship with their current clients. Check in with yourself right now: How effective are you at going back to the people who have purchased from you before and offering them additional products and services?

Another story about bonding is about Paul Rogers. When Robert Kiyosaki burst onto the scene with his best-seller *Rich Dad, Poor Dad*, Paul was teaching a seminar in St. Louis. Robert wasn't as well known as he is today, so Paul offered to give Robert a ride if he ever needed a ride when he was back in St. Louis. Robert's team of people said, "Well, we have people that handle that, so thanks, but no thanks." They took Paul's card, and that was the end of that.

Well, several months later, Paul got a call one night from Robert Kiyosaki's wife asking if he could pick up Robert at the airport because he needed a ride. So Paul went and picked up Robert, and in having that shared experience, Paul created a bond with Robert Kiyosaki. Paul then drove Robert wherever he needed to go in St. Louis over the next three days, creating an even deeper bond.

A few years later, when Robert appeared on *The Oprah Winfrey Show*, they went looking for some of Robert's successful students to appear with him. One of those successful students ended up being Paul Rogers. So Paul created a bond with Robert Kiyosaki by picking him up from the airport, which then evolved into Paul appearing on the *The Oprah Winfrey Show* with Robert Kiyosaki.

Bonding can (and should!) also happen with your friends and loved ones. Let me give you an example with my wife, Jarris. She was my first love. When we met, I was twenty-one, she was seventeen, and we fell in love. I went to her high school senior prom with her; eight months after meeting her, we eloped, and we've now been married for sixteen years. While we've had our ups and downs like probably any married couple has, we've successfully kept our marriage together because of the strong bond that we created very early in our relationship.

Ideas Into Action

Rapport reduces resistance. Rapport is the cornerstone of the sales process. You've probably heard the expression "people buy from people they like and trust," and rapport is the state of harmony that you can enter into with the prospect. And there are specific things that you can do that can cause the prospect to enter into the state with you.

When you're in the state of rapport with the prospect—when you're in harmony—they're much more likely to agree with you. You've probably had the opposite of this experience at times in your life, when you've talked with somebody and no matter what you said they wanted to disagree with you. Well, when you're in a state of rapport, they're far more likely to agree with you.

Key Points Review

- Believe in trust and rapport as the cornerstones of the sales process.

- Utilize the number one rapport-building technique: being present.

- Review the ideas presented here and develop your own ways to build rapport and trust.

- Use humor as a rapport-building tool.

- Use rapport and trust as a springboard to a deeper level of connection with your clients, called bonding.

Chapter 7

Identifying Needs

After we've built trust and rapport with the prospect, the next section of the sales mountain is to identify the customer's needs. Why take the time to do this, you ask? Why not just plow ahead with your presentation? Simple—What is the easiest way to persuade or influence someone? Discover what they want, then give it to them. How do you find out what someone wants? Ask questions.

We each have our own model of the world. As you are reading this book, your model of the world is different from my model of the world. Your model of the world is different from your manager's model of the world. Your client's model of the world is different from your model of the world. My six-year-old son's model of the world is different (a lot different!) from my model of the world. Want to connect with my six year-old-son? One way would be to talk about *Star Wars*, or *Indiana Jones*, or to discuss video games.

This can be thought of another way, too: We each have our own needs. My needs are different than your needs. Women's needs are different than men's needs. Your client's needs are different than your needs. We want to identify the customer needs. The easiest way that I've found to accomplish this is to, *prior to your sales presentation*, create a list of questions to ask the prospect to identify their true needs. Dr. Moine says that when you identify the true need of your prospect, your presentation becomes almost irresistible.

Key to Finding Needs: Questions

When most sales people deliver their presentation, they ask shoot-from-the-hip questions. In other words, they wing it, and hope that in the moment they'll be savvy enough to say or ask the right thing. The idea I am about to share you is so simple, yet so powerful, that if you just did this one thing, you'd be more effective on every presentation that you deliver for the rest of your life.

> *Think of the most powerful questions you could ask the prospect*
> **prior** *to the presentation. Then when meet the prospect, you've got*
> *your question prepared in advance.*

I want you to do this on your next presentation. Once you identify to whom you are going to deliver their presentation, identify the key questions to ask them *before the presentation*. One great way to research your customer is to do a Google search of their name. If they work for a company and you're selling business-to-business, also you should do a Google search of their company and their company website.

Your questions are meant to be *probing*, or attempting to dig below the surface to discover their true needs. There are probing questions and probing statements. A probing question would be this: "How much money do you have in your budget?" A probing statement elicits (you hope!) a more open-ended response: "Tell me about your current _____ situation."

At the sales presentation, don't launch immediately into a series of questions. This can appear pushy, and might even make the prospect feel (and thus act) defensive. Ask the prospect's permission first. Say to the prospect, "For me to best help you, Mr. Prospect or Mrs. Prospect, I need to ask you a few questions. Would that be okay?"

Trust me on this—the will say yes. Anytime I've ever asked that question of a prospect, they have always said yes. Human beings respond in predictable ways. I love questions where the prospect responds, "yes." (Unless, of course, I want the prospect to say "no!")

You could even go this far: "Prior to meeting with you today, I wrote down a list of questions, and with your permission I would like to go over those questions with you and take notes. Would that be okay?"

The prospect will of course agree, and you will win big points for appearing prepared, courteous, and professional.

If—after you *build trust and rapport* and launch immediately into *features and benefits*, thus skipping the *identifying customer needs* part—the prospect will be puzzled. The last car I purchased, the salesperson skipped **both** trust and rapport and identifying customer needs and went right into features and benefits. I only bought the car because I sold myself the car—I walked onto the lot and decided that I wanted to buy this particular car. Even though the salesperson did everything they could to mess up the sale, I still bought because I really wanted the car. In sales, you don't have to be good to earn a living. There are many average sales people who earn a decent living. But why just earn a living? Why not be extraordinary? And when you follow the sales mountain process, you can be extraordinary.

Examples of Probing Questions

Here are some examples of probing questions that you can ask:

> *What type of budget do you have to work with?*
>
> *How soon would you like to get started?*
>
> *Have you ever worked with a realtor before?*
>
> *Where do you currently buy your office supplies?*

Here are some examples of probing statements:

> *Tell me about your situation.*
>
> *Describe to me your dream job.*
>
> *How would you describe your credit?*

Each probing question or statement must, of course, fit your business, i.e., be appropriate to the situation. For instance, you wouldn't ask a prospect about their credit history if you are selling paper clips.

Exercise

Think of a prospect you will make a presentation to shortly. Now develop five probing questions:

1. _____

2. _____

3. _____

4. _____

5. _____

For this same prospect, develop five probing statements:

1. _____

2. _____

3. _____

4. _____

5. _____

Sometimes it's best to preframe a question with a story. Say you are a loan office who wants to know about a prospect's credit history. Rather than ask the rather blunt question, "How would you describe your credit?" you could tell the prospect a story, such as this: "Now, Mr. Prospect, before I ask you this next question, I want to share a quick story with you. I was talking on the phone with a client, and when I asked how they would describe their credit, they said pretty good. When I pulled their credit, however, I discovered that they had a bankruptcy that they obviously knew about. Because I didn't know about the bankruptcy, I put them into a certain loan product, and by the time I found out they had a bankruptcy, I had to stop that loan process and put them into another product. By that time the rates had gone up, costing them significant money. The reason why they didn't tell me about the bankruptcy is they were a little bit embarrassed about it. And I want you to know that our conversation today and all of our business dealings are confidential. I'll never share this with anyone else. I also want you to know that I've seen it all; I've seen perfect credit and I've seen not-so-perfect credit. The more honest you are with me, the more I can help you. Now how would you describe your credit?" (Of course, only tell a story like this if it's true!)

Do you see the power of that? We've preframed a delicate question with a story. Think about how you can apply this in your sales presentations.

Advanced Techniques

You also can attempt a trial close while asking probing questions. For example:

You:	"What's in your budget?"
Prospect:	"Oh, we have $2,000."
You:	"If I am able to submit a proposal under $2,000 that meets your needs, can you think of any reason why we won't be able to move forward?"

Isn't that powerful? I've found that when doing this, I close about 50% of all sales *before I've even gotten to the benefits-sharing stage of the presenation.*

Let me give you another advanced technique, learned from my mentor, Dr. Moine. It's called a "Buyer Fingerprint." Dr. Moine discovered that human beings make buying decisions in patterns. If you can identify the buying criteria of your prospect—in other words, how they make their buying decisions—in many cases you can close the sale during probing questions.

Let me give you an example. The first real estate property that my wife and I ever purchased was a condo in San Diego. We worked with an agent named was Frank Landy. At the time, my wife and I were on business in New Jersey. We didn't know any real estate agents in the San Diego area, so my wife called a toll free number she found on an ad for real estate. She got voice mail, so she hung up. Frank Landy posted that ad, and since toll-free numbers capture all numbers dialed to it, Frank called back and got my wife on the phone. That started the relationship.

When we got up to San Diego, we met face-to-face with Frank. After that initial meeting, I don't think I saw Frank again until some time later, when my wife had selected the final property. My wife met with Frank on numerous occasions, and they would look at property all over San Diego. At the time, we had a budget of $112,000 for a condo. Finally my wife found the property she wanted. Do you think this condo was under $112,000, at $112,000, or over $112,000? If you guessed over $112,000, you must have met my wife before, because the property was $129,500.

As we looked at the condo, I said to my wife, "Is this the one you want?" She said, "Yes."

"Is this the one that will make you happy?"

She said, "Yes."

And I said, "Great. Let's buy it."

So we stretched and we purchased it. Well, later on when my son was born, we wanted to buy a house. Frank was very personable and had maintained a relationship with us, so guess who we called to help us sell our condo and buy a home? Frank.

The three of us sat down again and agreed on a budget of $380,000. I didn't see Frank again until my wife had selected the property she wanted us to purchase. Do you think this home was under $380,000, at $380,000, or more than $380,000? If you guessed more than $380,000, you were right. We bought that property for $420,000. We stretched and we made it work.

This is the Buyer's Fingerprint. If you are a real estate agent and you wanted to help my wife and I find a home today, wouldn't it be valuable to know that the last three properties we purchased (there was one more after that!), we spent *more* than our budget? Wouldn't that be pretty valuable information to know in advance?

Obviously you would. Human beings make buying decisions in patterns. So, an advanced technique is to have probing questions to elicit somebody's buying criteria.

A final thought on Buyer's Fingerprint: This is an especially powerful dating technique. If you are reading this book and you're single and looking for that special someone, this technique is almost not fair. Go out on a date with the person you like and use the Buyer Fingerprint strategy. How? Simply ask a question like, "Tell me about the best date that you've ever been on." Then ask, "What was it about that date that made it so special?" As the person reveals more and more and more, they will soon tell you their strategy for falling in love.

Ideas Into Action

Remember my sales mantra: *Selling equals service*. When you take the time to identify a prospect's needs before jumping into your sales presentation, you are in a much better position to focus on providing value to the customer (as opposed to winning the sale). Probing questions and probing statements are your friends; they can help you learn so much about a prospect or client. Use questions systematically and extensively, and your business will grow by leaps and bounds.

Key Points Review

- What is the easiest way to persuade or influence someone? Discover what they want, then give it to them.

- How do you find out what someone wants? Ask questions.

- Probe for needs using both probing questions and probing statements.

- Utilize trial closes during the needs identification stage—many times, you will win the sale right there.

- Understand and utilize the Buyer Fingerprint strategy for all prospects.

Chapter 8

The Real Reason
People Buy

Time after time, I see sales people make two critical mistakes when delivering their presentation. One, they focus almost solely on what their product or service *does* (called its features), *rather than the benefits clients will receive from using the product or service*. Secondly, they only sell the benefits that *they* love. Don't sell the benefits you love. Sell the benefits that the *prospect* loves.

Ingrain this idea into your memory: *People buy benefits*. If you haven't taken the time before delivering your presentation to get clear on the benefits of your product or service, you are seriously hindering your ability to close more business.

Benefits build value in your presentation. Your prospect has a mental teeter-totter in their mind: on one side of the teeter-totter is price, on the other is value. Benefits help you stack more weight on the value side of the teeter-totter.

Before we jump into the meat of this chapter, let me give you now another key point: When selling to more than one person (for example, to a husband and a wife, or a committee), understand that each person has their own set of benefits that they are interested in. When people sell to my wife and I, often-times the salesperson will focus their attention on me and not on my wife. In most cases when this has happened, my wife has said, "I don't like the salesperson. I don't want to buy." The salesperson simply did not spend enough time building a rapport with my wife and understanding what benefits were important to *her*.

Types of Benefits

There are five different types of benefits:

Tangible benefits

Intangible benefits

The benefit of taking action

The consequences of not taking action

Benefit of the benefit

Let's review each.

Tangible benefits are real "things" like saving you money, making you money, decreasing employee turnover, and so on.

Intangible benefits are difficult to touch or measure, yet are still appealing. Intangible benefits include things like greater peace of mind, increased confidence, and so on. You can't always quite put your finger on intangible benefits, but they're very real benefits that people want.

Then there's the *benefit of taking action*, which is closely linked with the benefit of the consequences of not taking action. When I encourage people to create sales scripts (which I cover in Chapter 13), I let them know that the benefit of taking action by creating sales scripts is that they will close at a higher ratio, and thus make more money. The consequence of not taking action is that, for every presentation you deliver without having an effective sales script, you leave money on the table.

Currently our economy is in a downturn. In my public seminars I have been sharing with people that implementing these ideas is so important that your business survival may depend on it. Again, I am communicating the benefit of staying in business by clearly communicating the consequences of *not* taking action.

The last type of benefit is the *benefit of the benefit*. In many cases, this is the real reason why people buy.

Back to my sales training example: I'll say to a prospect, "Imagine you are now a sales champion. How will your life be different? What kind of car will you be driving?"

They usually say something like, "Oh, when I am a sales champion, I'll be driving this kind of car."

One of the benefits of being a sales champion is that you make more sales.

And then the benefit of the benefit of making more sales is you make more money. And the benefit of the benefit of the benefit is that you could drive the car that you want.

The Magic Word: "Imagine"

To substantially increase your sales, identify the prospect's benefit of the benefit. A real estate agent could say to a client, "Imagine you are living in your ideal home. Describe it to me." I love the word "imagine." It's a triggering phrase that stimulates the subconscious.

"Imagine that I have now sold your home. We've gotten the price that you wanted. What will this now allow you to do?"

The prospect's answer is their benefit of the benefit.

One tip to help you identify the benefit of the benefit is go to your satisfied clients that are enjoying the benefits of your products or service, and ask them this question: How have they benefited from what it is that you're offering?

Exercise

Make a laundry list of all of the benefits of your product or service:

_____   _____

_____   _____

_____   _____

_____   _____

_____   _____

_____   _____

_____   _____

_____   _____

_____   _____

Now each time you make a sales presentation, make sure that you've covered all of these key benefits.

The Power of Stories

One of my favorite ways to build value in a sales presentation is to tell success stories. Why? Simply because I believe nothing sells like success.

Here are some of the reasons why stories are so persuasive:

- Stories move people emotionally.
- Stories act as invisible selling.
- Stories suspend time.
- Stories can increase rapport.
- Stories can be humorous.

There are several different types of stories. You can:

- Tell your story.
- Tell your company's story.
- Tell stories of satisfied clients.
- Tell stories of clients who chose not to buy from you and now regret it.

Let me share a story with you to demonstrate the power of stories (!).

Many years ago, my wife Jarris was asked to be a bridesmaid in a wedding by her friend Nicole. Jarris had never been a bridesmaid before and was very excited. About six months prior to the wedding, Nicole invited Jarris out to lunch. At this point in our life, my wife and I had one child, our son Brandon, and we were talking about having a second child. During lunch, Nicole told Jarris a story about a time she was a bridesmaid in someone else's wedding. Apparently one of the other bridesmaids was pregnant and showing, which, Nicole explained, took away from the photos.

Now Nicole did not know that my wife and I were talking about having a second child at that time. When my wife came home from lunch with Nicole, she said, "I need to talk to you about something."

I said, "What's that?"

She told me the story how pregnant bridesmaid had ruined a bride's wedding photos. "So," my wife added, "we need to put our plans of having our second child on hold until after the wedding."

Wow—talk about impact! This short story Nicole told my wife altered my wife's and my behavior over the next several months. Look at the power, the influence, that short story had.

Let me share with you now one of my client success stories, one I regularly share during my seminars. It's about one of my star students named Arvee Robinson. I met Arvee at one of my seminars, and she signed up for my Protégé program, which included some one-to-one coaching time with me. During the coaching sessions, Arvee really connected with my messages. Arvee is one of the top trainers in the world, teaching people how to grow their business doing public speeches. She is very passionate about what she does, but at this time she was not producing very good business results. Why? Simply because she was uncomfortable selling and had a resistance to sales scripts.

Arvee became outstanding at implementing my number one distinction for sales greatest, which is to "stay in the conversation," (I write about this in depth in Chapter 15.) So Arvee continued with our coaching sessions, our Protégé calls; she even continued to return to the public seminars I was teaching at the time. Then one day, it all clicked for her. Suddenly she didn't just *like* sales, she *embraced* sales. She also embraced sales scripting. She began harnessing and using the power of sales scripting. Her income immediately shot up—she went from generating $4,000 a month in sales to $15–$20,000 a month in sales. With that increase in income, Arvee was soon able to realize one of her dreams of becoming a homeowner again. She had been renting for the previous eight years.

Pretty powerful, right?

Let me tell you another success story about another one of my star clients named David Laster. David sells insurance for AFLAC. When I met David, he was an average salesperson. He was highly motivated, though, so he drove a little over 125 miles one-way to attend one of my seminars. David really connected with my message and made a decision to stay in the conversation with me.

David signed up for the Protégé program. He currently has a lifetime membership with my organization. David continues to listen to the ideas that I share. Did this pay off? In 2007, David became a member of the prestigious AFLAC President's Club, reserved for the top eighty-five AFLAC reps nationwide out of 60,000. For being in the top eight-five, David won an all-expenses cruise to Italy and Monte Carlo. The following year, David again made the top eight-five and won a week-long, all-expenses-paid trip to Maui. David Laster is truly a sales superstar. Now that he has these skills, he can benefit from them for the rest of his life.

Ideas Into Action

Your sales career can take a dramatic positive turn by focusing on the key point of this chapter—that people buy based on benefits they will receive from the product, rather than the product's features (what it does). At every step of the sales process, be certain to focus on client benefits to move the prospect from being interested in your product or service to becoming a client.

Key Points Review

- People buy benefits—not features.

- There are five types of benefits. Know and use these.

- Use the word "imagine" to help get to your prospect's benefit of the benefit.

- Stories have power. Cultivate and use stories to help you close more business deals.

Chapter 9

Closing

Closing is my most requested topic for sales training presentations. Closing is one of the most profitable sales skills to have. It can be very easy when you know how, and once you have the skill, it's like knowing how to ride a bike: you can do it for the rest of your life.

But when you don't know how to close, closing can be one of the most frustrating and intimidating parts of sales. When I started off in sales and didn't know how to close, sales was frustrating. If I didn't make a sale, I didn't know what I did wrong; and even if I made a sale, I didn't know why and I couldn't repeat my success.

Fortunately I met Dr. Moine and learned his system for selling and closing, and I went from worst to first on my sales team in sixty days. This chapter will teach you the same closing secrets that enabled me to become a successful closer in just two months.

The Three Keys to Closing

When you don't know how to close, successful closing seems like something that happens rarely by accident. When you know the system for closing, successful closing begins to happen more regularly and predictably as your closing skills improve. This is because knowing the system lets you focus on improving each step in the closing process, increasing your odds of a successful close.

The three keys to successful closing are the same as the keys to the parts of sales:

- The inner game of closing
- The outer Game of closing
- Closing action

Now it's important to realize that just because you have a sales system doesn't mean you're going to close every sale. But it does mean your sales closing percentage will gradually improve. It's kind of like a baseball player improving their hitting skills.

I'm a San Francisco Giants fan, and I once heard a radio interview with Barry Bonds, all-time leader in single-season and career home runs, as well as career walks. Bonds is a polarizing figure because of his steroid use, and some people love him and some people hate him, but everyone agrees he was one of the greatest hitters of all time. The radio interviewer asked him a question to the effect of, "Isn't it frustrating when you hit a perfect line drive but it goes right to the second baseman for an out?" Bonds' reply was basically, "No, why should it be frustrating? My job as a hitter is to have a quality at-bat and hit the ball hard. Whether I get on base or not is another story."

In selling, your job is to deliver a quality sales presentation and ask for the sale. Whether your prospect buys or not can depend on other things besides your presentation—sometimes the line drive goes to the second baseman—but as long as you delivered the most quality presentation you could, you did your job. After your presentation, ask yourself, did I show up on time? Did I come from the heart? Did I deliver a quality presentation? Did I ask for the order? If the answer is yes, give yourself a pat on the back for doing a great job. If the answer is no, check to see whether or not you were following the three keys to closing successfully.

Closing Mindset

The first key is the inner game of closing, which involves your closing mindset. There are two extreme approaches to closing, like opposite ends of the pendulum. Most people subconsciously feel uncomfortable asking for money, which makes them hesitant to close and makes buyers hesitant to buy. At the other extreme, some people have an extremely aggressive mentality about closing, which can come across as pushy and turn buyers off.

The successful closing mindset contrasts with both of these extremes. A successful closer is confident enough in their closing system and their training rehearsal to be relaxed without being pushy. A successful closer begins from the mindset that *selling equals service*, that selling comes from honesty, integrity, and compassion, that selling is about leading and about moving people to action, and because they approach selling from this mindset, they have no reason to be ashamed about selling or afraid to ask for the close. A successful closer also knows that *selling is a system* and that if you follow the steps in the system, your close will come naturally without you needing to be pushy.

When you approach closing as a system, closing can be seen as *the section of the sales presentation where you ask for a commitment*. From this perspective, *the close is the natural conclusion to a well delivered presentation*. If you've planned and delivered a good presentation, you will naturally deliver a good close.

To plan an effective close, my system's approach is to decide before the presentation starts how you are going to close. Think of the presentation backwards, working from the close at the end back to the beginning. Imagine how the close is going to go. Think about how you are going to explain each step. Decide in advance what you are going to say. And once you've decided what you're going to say, *practice, practice, practice* until you can deliver your close naturally without thinking about it, consistently, time after time.

This consistency is key to successful closing. The most successful people I have ever met in closing did the same thing over and over again. I watched my mentor Dante Perano close about fifty times. Each close was exactly the same! Human beings respond in patterns. When you find a pattern that moves people to action you can repeat the steps over and over and over and move many people to action.

To achieve this kind of consistency, you must adopt a mindset to *embrace sales scripting*. Dr. Moine defines a script as words in sequence that have meaning, and he places a strong emphasis on using scripts, as do other leading sales trainers. Some salespeople don't like to use scripts because they worry about sounding canned or rehearsed or they believe that a script is beneath them. I use scripts because they work. They are good for me and good for the customer or client. Scripts are the easiest, most effective way to move someone to action.

Planning Sales Scripts

Scripts have two components:

- Language
- Structure

The language includes your words, tonality, speech rate, body language, and pauses.

The structure is the order of your script. It is the sequence. A great example I mentioned at the beginning of Section II is the script sequence a waiter or waitress at the Olive Garden uses. When you arrive at the Olive Garden, the people serving you will ask you a series of questions in a specific order:

1. How many are in your party
2. Can I get you a beverage?
3. Would you like an appetizer?
4. What would you like to eat?
5. How is your meal?
6. Would you like any dessert or coffee?

Now notice that this order has a logical step-by-step sequence. It wouldn't make sense for the waitress to ask you for dessert as soon as you walk in the door. Similarly, it doesn't make sense to try to close a sales presentation before the appropriate time.

A full sales presentation follows this sequence:

1. Establish trust and Rapport
2. Identify customer needs
3. Share the benefits

4. Close

5. Handle objections

6. Follow up

It's important to be conscious of where the close fits within this sequence and to plan your close accordingly. This enables you to set the stage for a close that naturally follows from a well-delivered presentation. It also prevents you from trying to close before you've laid the groundwork for a successful close.

Planning Closing Scripts

When you get to the close, the close itself also has a specific natural sequence. Being aware of this sequence when you plan your close helps you script it more effectively.

The sequence of an effective close generally includes these elements in this order:

1. Price

2. What is included

3. Risk reducers: discounts, guarantees, or warranties

4. Reward strengtheners: bonuses

5. Urgency builders: incentives for buying today, consequences of not taking action

6. Call to action: asking for the order

Following these steps, you wait for the prospect's response. Either they will buy or they will make an objection. We'll come back to objection handling in the next chapter. First let's talk some more about the close.

Closing Techniques

Within the structure of your sales scripts and your closing scripts, there are a variety of closing techniques you can use. These include techniques for setting up the close as well as techniques for delivering the close itself.

Preframe

One way to set the stage for your close earlier in your presentation is to let someone know in advance what is going to happen so they're already expecting a close. This called *preframing* the close: it creates the framework for the close.

I often preframe closes when I'm delivering a one-on-one or group presentation. For instance I might say early in the presentation, "I have two outcomes for our presentation. My first outcome is to share some great ideas with you. My second outcome is to share with you how my ongoing coaching program works. I will give you all the details at the end of our meeting."

There are many variations of this technique you can use. For example, a financial planner might preframe a close by saying before an appointment, "For me to best help you I need you to have your taxes from the last two years ready for our appointment. Can you have that ready?" Another way of preframing a close before an appointment would be to say something like, "In order for me to meet with you I need you and your spouse at the appointment. Will that work for you?"

Trial close

A powerful variation of close preframing is a technique called a *trial close*. Here you get someone to agree early in the presentation that if you can meet certain conditions during your presentation, they will agree to buy. For example, a financial consultant might say, "If I can reduce your monthly payments and get you $10,000 in cash at close would you like to refinance your mortgage?"

Ask

When you get to the close, the most basic form of the close is *asking* a simple question. An everyday example is asking someone, "Would you like to go to lunch?" As this illustrates, closing is something we all do every day. It doesn't have to be hard.

Assumption close

When asking for a close, you can often sidestep resistance by wording your close on the assumption that the sale has been made, called an *assumption close*. An example is to close by asking, "Which credit card would you like to use today?"

Alternate of choice close

A similar closing technique that bypasses resistance is to word the close in a way that limits the prospect's options to a set of choices that both assume a sale, called an *alternate of choice close*. Here are a few examples:

> "I am looking at my calendar. I am available on the second or the ninth. What would work best for you?"
>
> "We accept Visa, American Express, Discover, or MasterCard. Which card would you like to use?"
>
> "We can do a 3 month or 4 month listing. What would work best for you?"
>
> "We can do a 15-year or 30-year loan. What would work best for you?"
>
> "You can buy 1 month of service or 12 months. If you buy 12 months you will receive a discount. What would work best for you?"

Order form close

Another way to close effectively is to walk your prospect through the close by providing an order form, called an *order form close*. In this technique, you simply give the prospect an order form and walk them through filling it out. This involves simple direct commands worded as instructions, like, "Put your name here," "Jot down your mailing address," and "Put your credit card here."

Sympathy close

Sometimes you can strengthen your close by emphasizing another element of your sales presentation. For instance, you can build on rapport and appeal to the benefit of helping others by using the *sympathy close*. An example of a sympathy close is wording the close as an appeal for help. For example, "It would really help me out if you could buy some cookies from my daughter for the Girl Scouts. Most people are buying five boxes. Could you buy at least two?"

Contrast close

When you're stating your price and you want to emphasize savings, an effective technique is the *contrast close*. This is a close that stresses the contrast between the price you're asking and the benefits you're offering. I once saw an ad that was selling a $1,000,000 home for $775,000. Another example is a $6 Burger at Carl's Jr. Think about other ways you can use contrast in your presentation and your close, either to emphasize price or some other value you're offering.

Leverage close

Another way of closing is to emphasize the negative consequences that come from not accepting the call to action, called a *leverage close*. This is a common technique with collection agencies. They point out the consequences if you don't pay. Insurance salesman Ben Feldman used this technique effectively to portray the consequences of not buying insurance.

Scarcity close

A similar way to stress the consequences of not taking action is the *scarcity close*. An example of a scarcity close is saying something like, "We only have one left. Would you like to get it?" You often see scarcity closes used in TV ads for offers that are not available in stores or are available for a limited time only.

Ask and be silent close

A technique that works well in conjunction with most of the other closing techniques discussed here is the *ask and be silent close*. In this close you ask a question for commitment and be silent.

A good illustration of this close is the way the Girl Scouts close sales. When a Girl Scout closes a sale, she asks you, "Would you like to buy some Girl Scout Cookies?" Then she waits for your answer. This tosses you the "hot potato" and puts the pressure on you instead of her.

Realize that your prospect is facing this same pressure after you deliver a close, and learn to get comfortable waiting in silence for their response. Concentrating on holding your fist to keep yourself from talking is one way to help you manage any anxiety you may experience during this phase of the close.

The advantage of this technique is that it helps you avoid one of the most common closing mistakes salesmen make. Some salesmen get so nervous after asking for the order that they keep on talking and lose a sale they would otherwise have made. Remaining silent after asking for the order avoids this problem.

Learning to ask and be silent is one of the most important closing techniques to learn and apply. When I close one-on-one, I always use this technique.

Ideas Into Action

To put the ideas in this chapter into action, I encourage you to commit to three main actions:

First, begin using affirmations to cultivate the mindset that ***the close is the natural conclusion to a well delivered presentation*** and to ***embrace sales scripting***.

Second, write down the script for the close of your main sales presentation.

Third, get in the habit of practicing your script regularly by recording it and listening to it, rehearsing it aloud, practicing it with a partner, and practicing it live with prospects.

Key Points Review

- The big idea from this chapter is to prepare in advance how you are going to close and then go and implement.

- The three keys to closing are Inner Game, Outer Game, and Action.

- You can win the closing Inner Game by developing the mindset that ***the close is the natural conclusion to a well delivered presentation*** and by ***embracing sales scripting***.

- Sales scripts have two main components: language and structure.

- You can script the structure of your close by identifying the elements you need to include (such as price, what is included, and discounts), and presenting them in a logical order.

- When it comes to wording the language of your close, there are a variety of techniques available that you should become familiar with and practice.

- One of the most important techniques you should learn is to ***ask and be silent***.

- Practice, practice, practice your closing script until it becomes natural.

Chapter 10

The Elegant Dance: Objections

Many salespeople cite overcoming objections as the most challenging part of the sales process. Needless to say, the sales superstar must be able to comfortably overcome objections to dramatically increase his or her sales. Because when a person is uncomfortable handling an objection, they often become nervous in the close. When they're nervous during the close, this negatively impacts their ability to influence the prospect.

In this chapter of *The System*, I will share with you powerful idea after powerful idea on how to effortlessly anticipate and handle every objection that comes up.

Objections: A Definition

Let's start off by defining the term objection. An objection is a reason the prospect gives for not buying. Most objections are not true. For example, a prospect may say that they don't have time to complete the sale; they do have the time, they just don't want to move forward. Many times they say they don't have the money . . . yet they have the money. Many times they say they need to talk about it with someone else . . . when in reality they can make the decision themselves.

Why then do people give objections, especially untrue ones?

I believe the most common reason is out of habit. Author and speaker Mark Victor Hansen says our habits determine up to 90 percent of our behavior. Over time, people simply fall into the habit of not making decisions. So when you get to the end of a presentation, and you ask the prospect to make a decision, oftentimes they respond in their normal pattern of giving an objection.

Please note that "objection handling" is a sales training term; never use the word objection with your prospect. Instead, use the term *concern*.

Don't say: "Is that your only objection?"

Say: "Is that your only concern?"

At the end of your presentation, you are going to ask for the order. After you ask for the order, you are going to be silent. For example, you would say, "How do you feel about moving forward today?" Then remain silent. It's okay if no one speaks for a moment; part of the language of influence is silence. When you remain silent, the prospect must do one of three things: say yes, say no, or give an objection. I always close the sale by asking for the order and being silent. The prospect always responds by saying one of those three things: yes, no, or an objection.

Prediction is a form of power. If they say yes, write up the order. If they say no, they've said no. If they give an objection, handle it with one of the techniques in this chapter or one of the techniques you already know.

Here's another way to think about objections: think of it as a "hot potato." Asking for the order and remaining silent is like tossing the prospect a hot potato. When they give an objection, they are tossing back to you the hot potato. When you have the hot potato, you want to do one of two things: You either want to give them back the hot potato, or give them back the hot potato and ask for the order. You don't have to say the perfect thing, just say *something*. I call this process "elegantly dancing with the prospect." I don't believe in using high pressure, arm-twisting techniques. I believe in elegantly dancing with the prospect. When the prospect gives an objection, you simply start the dance by using objection-handling techniques.

Here's still another way to think about objections: Handling them is really a form of negotiation. When you go to a car lot to buy a car, after the test drive the salesperson might say, "Would you like to buy the car?"

You say, "How much is it?"

They say, "It's $25,000."

Do most people immediately say, "Great, I'll take it!"? Most likely you don't.

Most likely, you will say, "I'm interested in buying the car... but not for $25,000. I'd be willing to pay $18,000."

When you say $18,000 to the salesperson, do you expect them to say, "Great! I'll go let my manager know that we are going to sell you the car for $18,000"?

No, of course not.

They go to their manager, then come back and say something like, "I spoke with the big boss, and the big boss said at $25,000, we're already taking a loss on this car. But we really want to sell you the car, so he's willing to go $24,500." And thus the dance has started.

You expect this back-and-forth when you go to purchase a car at a car dealership. Objection handling is no different. So, when you go in to the close, it is very natural for a prospect to give an objection just like when you are negotiating. Objection handling is a form of negotiation.

Objection Handling in the Real World

The great thing about becoming an expert at handling objections is that objections come up in all areas of life, professional and personal. Here's an example of real world influence. Sometimes when I pick up my son from kindergarten, he'll get into the car, then say, "Dad, can we go to McDonald's today?"

"Not today, son."

"C'mon, Dad. Just this once."

"Brandon, we went yesterday."

"Oh, c'mon."

Usually we banter back and forth, back and forth. Sometimes I take him, sometimes I don't. That's real world influence.

Key Point

Don't take objection handling to an extreme; in other words, don't make it a competition between the prospect and yourself. Instead, consider selling as a mental chess game. Part of chess is anticipating your opponent's next move. I do not view sales as a competition against the prospect, but I am fully aware of the "game" we are playing.

Common Objections

Any industry typically has seven to twelve common objections. This is great news. Why? You not only can choose to improve your objection handling techniques and responses, you can prepare ahead of time for common objections. Here are many of the objections common to almost all industries, products, and services:

- I need to think about it.
- I don't have any money.
- I need to talk it over with someone.
- Can you fax me some information?
- I don't have the time.
- Your price is too high.
- I am already working with someone.
- We already tried it and it didn't work.
- I'm not interested.

Exercise

You will want to identify and prepare for the common objections in your industry. For now, simply grab a pen and jot down the common objections in your industry. Use the list of objections just provided as a beginning.

_____

_____

_____

_____

_____

_____

_____

_____

_____

_____

Now, create a folder in Microsoft Word called "Objections" and add a laundry list inside a Word doc of all the common objections that you have in your industry.

Addressing Objections

Ways to address objections include the following:

1. Story
2. Non-stated
3. Question
4. Solve the problem
5. Isolate the objection
6. Bring out the objection
7. Script
8. Investigative selling
9. Before it comes up
10. Show the benefits
11. Reduce the risk
12. Be unreasonable
13. Negotiate
14. What would need to happen…?
15. Intuition

Let's review each of these.

Number 1: Story

One of the most powerful ways to handle an objection is with a story. Stories not only act as invisible selling tools, they also suspend time. Identify true stories that address the objection. One way to start off a story is by saying, "That reminds me of a story of a client who was in a similar situation. Let me share with you what they did." The punch line to the story would be the prospect ended up buying your product or service and then enjoyed the great benefits received.

Number 2: Non-stated

Oftentimes the true objection is a non-stated objection, where the prospect states an objection but it isn't the real one. In other words, the prospect says, "I don't have the money" when in reality their real concern is the need to discuss the situation with their spouse before they make a buying decision. Or they prospect says, "I need to think it over." Does this prospect really need more time? Maybe the real issue is that they are going to meet with another salesman selling the same product.

Number 3: Question

You can answer an objection with a question. For example, if the prospect says the price is too high, you could then say, "By too high, what exactly do you mean?" After you ask that question, remain silent. Here are two other examples:

Prospect:	"The price is too high."
You:	"How much too much is it?"
Prospect:	"The price is too high."
You:	"Compared to what?"

Here are questions to a prospect's "I don't have the time" objection.

Prospect:	"I don't have the time."
You:	"When will you have the time?"
Prospect:	"I don't have the time."
You:	"On a scale of one-to-ten, how motivated are you to move forward?"
Prospect:	"I don't have the time."
You:	"What do you mean by that?"

Number 4: Solve the Problem

You can also handle an objection by simply solving the problem. Here's an example:

Prospect:	"I don't have any money to invest."

You:	"I can appreciate that, Mr Prospect. Let me ask you a question: if you had the money to invest, would you like to get started?"
Prospect:	"Well, sure."
You:	"Great, here's what I can do for you. I can offer you a free consultation. During the consultation, I'll look at your finances and see if we can free up any money you are currently spending. I recently met with a client and we freed up $150 to invest on a monthly basis. If I could help you free up some money to invest, would that interest you?" (Remember, ask, then remain silent.)

Number 5: Isolate the Objection

Isolating the objection is one of my favorite techniques. It's not only easy to learn but also very effective. Here's an example:

Prospect:	"I don't have the money."
You:	"I can appreciate that. Other than the money, is there anything else that's preventing you from moving forward today?"
Prospect:	"I don't have the time."
You:	"Other than the time, is there anything else that is preventing you from moving forward today?"

Every time the prospect states an objection, you simply respond back with a set language pattern: "Other than (blank) is there anything else that is preventing you from moving forward today?" You have then isolated the core objection, and can move forward by overcoming that one element.

Number 6: Bring Out the Objection

The opposite of isolating the objection, bringing out the objection is another simple yet very powerful technique. Oftentimes the true objection is a non-stated objection. Many times the prospect will not reveal the true objection. Each objection they give you in this case becomes a stall, not an objection. When you use this technique, it encourages the prospect to be honest with you.

Here's an example:

Prospect:	"I don't have the money."
You:	"I understand. So, what you are saying is you don't have the money, is that correct?"
Prospect:	"Yes, that's correct."
You:	"I'm sure you have some other concerns before moving forward. Do you mind sharing what those other concerns are?" (Then remain silent.)

Or this example:

Prospect:	"I need to think about."
You:	"I understand. Other than thinking about it, I am sure that you have some other concerns before moving forward. Do you mind sharing what those concerns are?" (Then remain silent.)

Number 7: Answer an Objection with a Script

I suggest that you develop scripted responses to each objection. Here's an example:

Prospect:	"I need to speak to my wife first before making this decision."
You:	"I understand. So if your wife says yes, does that mean you'll move forward?"
Prospect:	"Yeah, I guess so."
You:	"Great, let me ask you a different question. What if she says 'no'?"
Prospect:	(In most cases.) "Well, I'll do it anyway."
You:	"Congratulations! You're going to love attending my seminar."

I have used this script over and over again for the prospect that tells me that they need to talk it over with their husband or wife. In about 30 percent of the cases, I get the sale.

Number 8: Investigative Selling

No matter what the prospect says, you say, "Tell me more about that." If the prospect says, "I don't have the money," you say, "Tell me more about that." If the prospect says, "I don't have the time," you say, "Tell me more about that."

One of my star clients, Joe Anandoah, loves sales. Joe sells several things, including an awesome air purifier. Here's a conversation Joe had one day with a prospect:

Joe:	"Would you like to buy one of my air purifiers?"
Prospect:	"I don't have the money."
Joe:	"Tell me more about that."
Prospect:	"Well, it's not actually about the money."
Joes:	"What is it then?"
Prospect:	"It's my wife."
Joe:	"Tell me more about that."
Prospect:	"Well, I bought two air purifiers, and neither one of them worked. They are both sitting in my garage. I'm not using either one. If I buy another air purifier, my wife will be upset with me."
Joe:	"Where did you buy the purifiers from?"
Prospect:	"XYZ Corporation."
Joe:	"That's a very reputable company. Have you tried to return them? I mean, if they don't work, I am sure they will take them back."
Prospect:	"I haven't tried that."
Joe:	"Well, why don't you do this: Call the company and see if they will take them back. If they will, will you then buy my air purifier?"
Prospect:	"Let me see what I can do."

The company did take those air purifiers back, and Joe did close the sale—all by handling an objection using the "tell me more about that" (investigative selling) technique.

Number 9: Answering the Objection Before It Comes Up

This is one of the most powerful objection handling techniques. You simply reverse-engineer (begin with the end in mind) your sales presentation by anticipating the key objections a prospect might bring up, and then address the objections during your sales presentation. For example, you anticipate that the prospect is going to need to think about the decision. You could address this in the body of the presentation the following way:

> You: "Mr. Prospect, when it comes to making decisions, what I've found is successful people make decisions quickly and rarely change them. Unsuccessful people take a long time to make a decision and change them rapidly. Today, I am going to share a solution that I believe will help your company save time and money. At the end of my presentation, I am going to ask that you make one of two decisions: to either move forward or not move forward. Does that sound fair?"
>
> Prospect: "Yes."

One time I was given a sales presentation to purchase a timeshare. At the beginning of the presentation, the salesman said, "At our company we don't negotiate price. The price is the price. However, when we deliver the presentation, we do offer same-day incentives. So if you do purchase today, we have some incentives to offer you that are only good today. Does that sound fair?"

What else could I say except, "That sounds fair to me."

This is brilliant scripting—they handled two objections (price, thinking it over) early on in the presentation before I was able to state them.

Often when you are selling a car or selling real estate or a product like a timeshare, the prospect wants to negotiate. By saying during the presentation, *we don't negotiate here in our company; the price is the price*, that eliminates a likely your-price-is-too-high objection. Please note that the *price is the price* does *not* mean the *price is the price*; that's simply an advanced way of handling the objection before it comes up.

Think about how you could incorporate the technique of handling an objection before it comes up by addressing it in the body of the presentation. As you learn and master these techniques, they will make you more effective on every single sales presentation that you deliver for the rest of your life.

Number 10: Share the Benefits

Objections provide a great opportunity to share the benefits. If the prospect says that they don't believe insurance is a good investment, for example, you can then share with them all the great benefits of why highly successful people own insurance.

Number 11: Reduce the Risk

This means that you change the offer. Let's say you are asking for a six-month coaching commitment, and the prospect says, "The price is too high." Reduce the risk by saying, "I understand. Perhaps we could take a smaller step first. Instead of working on a six-month agreement, why don't we do a three-month agreement? Sound good?"

By changing the offer, you've reduced the prospect's risk, overcome their objection (you hope!), and given yourself a strong opportunity to close the sale.

I used this technique to land a sales training contract with Wells Fargo Mortgage. My inside salesperson contacted them to book an appointment for me to be a guest speaker at one of their branch manager meetings. The Vice President of Sales for Southern California, a woman named Martha Philips, said, "I am not familiar with Eric Lofholm. I wouldn't be interested in him speaking to our team." Now this was early on in my career when I was just getting started. Still, I had trained my appointment setters to use the following script:

My team: "Martha, I understand how you feel about this. Why don't I have the president of our company, Eric Lofholm, stop by your office for only five minutes? He'll share with you how your company can benefit from what he has to offer. Sound good?"

Martha: "Okay. Please have Eric visit my office."

I went and met Martha. I was prepared. Not only did I have my scripts ready, I also started sharing stories with her. The reason I started telling Martha stories is because stories suspend time. Remember, I had only asked for, and been given, five minutes. Forty-five minutes into the appointment, I pointed at my watch—believe me, this is a true story—and said, "Martha, I have to run, I have another appointment that I need to get to."

Martha liked me and she booked me for the speaking engagement . . . which ultimately led to a $15,000 sales training contract. All by reducing her risk.

Think about how you can use this technique in your sales career. If you are a real estate agent and asked for a listing appointment yet the prospect resisted, you could simply say, "How about I stop by for only five minutes and drop off some valuable information about property values in your area? If, after we meet, you feel comfortable scheduling an appointment, we can talk about doing that at a later time. Sound good?"

And all of sudden, the prospect says, "Yeah, you can come over for five minutes and drop off some valuable information for me." Now, you wouldn't want to do that for every presentation. But in some instances, it makes sense

Here's another example. I recently had an opportunity to do some training for a company, yet they were hesitant about bringing me out to train them. So I said, "How about this: I'll fly to Hawaii, at my expense, and I will do a free training for you that I would normally charge $10,000 for. I won't promote my website. I won't sell anything. In fact, I won't even bring my business cards. I will just come out and give you a free training. I will audition for you, and after you hear the quality of my training, if you feel comfortable we can move forward with some other sales training."

Of course they agreed—how could they say no? It cost them nothing to get a free $10,000 training program. Did it work out for me? After my program, I received a standing ovation, and am now an approved Corporate Trainer for their company. All because I used a technique called reduce the risk.

Number 12: Be Unreasonable

How? Make an unreasonable request. For example, if a prospect says they don't have the money, tell them to get a second job so they can purchase your product or service, or suggest that they sell their car. These are unreasonable requests, and in some cases that would be an appropriate way to handle that objection.

Here's an example. I wanted my wife to attend a seminar with me. Jarris said, "When is it?" When I gave her the dates, she said, "I can't make it that weekend."

"Why not?"

"I not only already have plans to take the kids to see your parents, I already bought the plane tickets," Jarris argued.

I shrugged. "No problem. Why don't you visit my parents another weekend?"

My wife explained that the tickets were bargain tickets, and thus nonrefundable.

Now, for most people that objection would be un-overcome-able. But not for me. I said to my wife, "This seminar is too important to miss. I would like you to go see my parents another weekend and repurchase the tickets."

She then said, "If it is that important to you, then I'll do it."

In this case I overcame the objection—the tickets are nonrefundable—by being unreasonable. Sometimes you can overcome an objection by being unreasonable.

Number 13: Negotiate

You can change the deal by negotiating. We're not going to reduce the risk here, we are going to keep the deal the same, but change the terms. "If I lower the price by 5 percent, will you move forward today?"

Number 14: What will need to happen ...?

You can also close the sale by asking this question: What would need to happen in order for you to move forward today?

There are many ways to apply this particular objection-handling technique. Years ago when I used to promote seminars for Tony Robbins, I would be at a company and they would agree to purchase tickets for anyone on their team interested in attending the seminar. So I would do the presentation, and let's say ten people decided they wanted to go. Well, the tickets are $229 each, so I now have ten registration forms, no payment, and the company owes me $2,290. I would then go back to the company and say, "Okay, ten people signed up. What's the process in getting a check cut?" Usually the company would say something like, "We need to send it back to corporate, which will take about two weeks for you to get a check."

I learned, as you probably have, that if you walk out of that office without the check, there's a good possibility you won't ever it. So I would simply say,

"What would need to happen in order to get a check cut today?" They'd say something like, "Well, we'd have to go talk it over with the Vice President, and they'd have to approve it." I'd say, "Great. I'll have a seat in the lobby. Let me know what the answer is."

Now they might say, "It's impossible to get a check cut today. We don't even have the checks physically here."

Then I would solve the problem. I'd say, "Well, I am sure that you have a way of making a payment in the event that something comes up and you need to make the payment today. Do you have a company credit card?"

They'd say, "Well, yes, we have American Express."

Then I would simply say, "Great, we accept American Express. I'll wait here while you go get the card."

Number 15: Intuition

Sometimes, when you are with a prospect, the right response perfect for that moment will simply come to you. I won't have trained you on the response here. In fact, it's not one that you even know. You simply realize in the moment what is the best thing to say, and you say it. I call this one intuition.

Putting It All Together

Let me share a story with you about one of my star clients, Mandy Pratt, who made a decision to master these skills. She was delivering a sales presentation over the phone selling a high-priced, wealth-building program. The program was around $6,000. Here's how the dance with the prospect went:

Mandy:	"How do you feel about moving forward?"
Prospect:	"I don't have the money."
Mandy:	"Other than the money, is there anything else that's preventing you from moving forward?"
Prospect:	"Well, it's actually not the money. It's my husband."
Mandy:	"Tell me more about that."
Prospect:	"Well, I bought a program similar to this a few years ago without first talking it over with my husband. The program

didn't work and we were out several thousands dollars, and my husband was very upset with me. I'm concerned that if I buy this program tonight, my husband might be unhappy with me."

Mandy: "I understand. So you want to find out how your husband feels about this before you make an investment in the program?"

Prospect: "Exactly."

Mandy: "Let me ask you a question—is your husband home tonight?"

Prospect: "Yes."

Mandy: "Let's put him on the line and I will share with him that you have an interest in the program and that you want to hear if he has any concerns before moving forward. How does that sound?"

Prospect: "I can do that."

The woman's husband joined the conversation.

Mandy: "Sir, I was talking with your wife who is very interested in one of our programs. This is what the program is. It costs $6,000. She said that you both had a bad experience before and she don't want to do anything without you first knowing what she was doing and secondly, that you felt that that was a good decision. We wanted to know how you feel about this?"

After talking for a few more minutes, the husband said, "Listen, if this is what my wife wants to do, she has my blessing." Mandy made a $6,000 sale. Her commission was 20 percent, which meant that she earned a $1,200 commission on that single sale. More importantly, Mandy has the skill set to "elegantly dance with the prospect." She is currently in her thirties and she will have that skill set for the rest of her life, making her hundreds of thousands of dollars in increased commissions.

Ideas Into Action

It's possible that the techniques in this one chapter could earn you an additional $100,000 in commissions between now and the end of your career. Also, if you have a team of people that work for you or underneath you, be sure to share these techniques with them, and you could multiply your override commissions.

Key Points Review

- Sales superstars must be able to comfortably overcome objections to dramatically increase his or her sales.

- Never use the term "objection" with a client; use "concern."

- Prepare in advance for common objections.

- Master the objection-handling techniques presented here.

Chapter 11

The Fortune in the Follow-up

Here's a sales secret I want to share with you (please don't tell too many others, this is one of those closely-guarded sales secrets): The prospect doesn't always buy when he or she is supposed to. Sometimes they want to wait. Now, this waiting is often a stall, meaning that you haven't shown enough value. But other times this waiting has a legitimate purpose, such as preparing a purchase order number. What must you do when the prospect doesn't buy? Follow up!

I can't tell you how important the concept of following up with a prospect can be to your business. Let me give you a quick story. Many years ago, the company I was working for hired a professional trainer to do sales. He was a great trainer, a likable guy, and everyone thought that he was going to make a killing doing sales. But he flopped. One day, I asked him about a big meeting he had had with a prospect. "They can't make up their mind," he said. I asked him when he was going to contact them again. He said, "When they call me." Wrong answer! A true sales professional would continue to touch base with the prospect in a professional, courteous way—he or she wouldn't wait for the prospect to call.

In this chapter, let's cover ways to make you a fortune in the follow-up.

The $50,000 Idea

I call my primary follow-up idea the "Fifty Thousand Dollar Idea." If you implement this one idea to your business, I believe that it will generate an additional $50,000 in increased commissions to you above and beyond what you would have already earned had you not applied this principle.

Now for some of you reading this, this idea will be far more valuable to you than $50,000. This one idea has been far more valuable to me than $50,000, and I still have a thirty-seven year run left in me! When it's all said and done, it will probably end up meaning many millions of dollars in increased sales.

Here's the follow-up mindset and $50,000 idea that I use in my business. Let's say that you delivered an effective presentation, you asked for the order, they gave you an objection, you elegantly danced with the prospect, and they said, "Well listen, I still need you to follow up with me." They ask you to call them on Tuesday at four o'clock, so you call them at the appointed time and you get their voicemail. You leave them a message and ask them to call you, and they don't call you. So now you're in a dilemma. The prospect asked you to follow up with them, which you did, and they did not return your call. So you're in this question, there's this voice in the back of your head, you're having this conversation with yourself, and the conversation is, "Should I call again, or should I not call? Should I call again, or should I not call?"

Somehow you muster up the courage and call again, only to leave them another voicemail. Again they don't call you back. Now you're really in a dilemma; you've left two voicemails, and in your mind, you're going, "Look, I want to follow up, but I don't want to bother the prospect." Has that ever happened to you? It's happened to me! What do you do? My philosophy—and this is the Fifty Thousand Dollar Idea—is to follow up, follow up, follow-up, *until they buy or die*. In other words, keep working to take the sale to a conclusion of a "yes" or a "no." I never think that I am bothering a prospect when I follow up with them. Think about it—I'm calling them to share information and help them make more money every month for the rest of their life. That's not bothering a prospect. When I am calling a prospect, I'm adding value. My mindset is this: They're still interested, it's just that life got in the way.

One time, I was following up with a prospect that had expressed a sincere interest in having me speak to his him. I called him, he didn't call me back. I called him again; he didn't call me back. I must've called him five or six times without him returning my call. I reviewed my philosophy to follow up, follow up, follow up until they buy or die, so I continued to call him about once a month. Six months later, he finally returned my phone call, and said, "Eric, I appreciate your follow-up and I'm sorry for not returning your call. My wife and I just got a divorce." It turns out that they were business partners and his whole world had been turned upside down. It wasn't that he wasn't interested in me speaking to his team, it's that life had thrown him a curve ball.

Every once in a while you will run into someone who, after you have called numerous times, will say something like, "Why do you keep calling me? I thought you'd get the hint after the fifteenth phone call." I suggest that you simply say, "Well, the last time we spoke, you shared with me that you were interested, so I was just following up based on your interest. If you're no longer interested, then I won't call you anymore." Then you just leave it at that.

Here are several key points to remember regarding staying in touch with someone:

- Always stay polite and maintain rapport even when leaving numerous phone messages.
- Consider leaving different messages.
- Use humor if you can. For example, you might say something like, "Bob, I'm following up with you. I've called you a few times now and I have your file on my desk. I can't take the file off my desk until I hear back from you. Please call me to let me know your thoughts regarding moving forward." That's a nice way to let the prospect know that you're going to continue to call them until the two of you connect.

KEY POINT

1. Most people rate themselves a five or less on a scale of 1-10 in the area of follow-up. How would you rate yourself on a scale of 1-10? _____

2. What can you do immediately to become a "10"? _____

_____

Ways to Follow Up

There are many ways to follow up with a prospect. You could follow up with a phone call, you could follow up with a text message; you could follow up with an instant message; you could follow up with an email; you could follow up by doing a walk-in. If you have tried one way with no results, try another.

Above all, be creative. Here's an example where I turned feeling bad about failing to call a prospect back into a closed deal. I met a client in San Diego who expressed interest in me writing some sales scripts for them. But I failed to do the proper follow-up; I was supposed to call the prospect but didn't. I then felt guilty about not doing what I had promised to do. Next thing I know, I have an opportunity to go to San Diego on other business. I debated about whether or not to contact the client I had "let down," as I saw it. But then I thought, "You know, Mark expressed interest. If he still has a need, perhaps he's going to be more interested in getting that need met rather than the fact that I didn't follow up in a timely fashion."

So I called Mark and told him this: "Mark, I'm coming to your area and I have an open day. Let me cut you a super deal, so that you can get your sales scripts done, and I can take advantage of a dead day. What do you say we move forward?" He agreed to hire me. Even though I felt guilty, I was able to close the sale and Mark was able to enjoy the benefits of the scripts I wrote for him.

Here's a story about fear. Yes, I experience fear just like everyone else. I was calling on a real estate Internet marketing company in San Diego called z57.com. I had done business with them before, and I was calling to be a guest speaker at one of their sales meetings. Dave Baird was in charge of the meeting. I called up Dave and he expressed interest in having me speak, but we didn't actually book the date. He asked me to follow up with him. So I followed up with him and I got his voicemail. He didn't return my call. This happened at least three more times. Now his office was about fifteen minutes from mine, so I thought, "You know what? I'm just going to drive over there, show up at his office, and attempt to book the appointment."

I got into my car, drove over to his office, and then in the parking lot I started having a conversation with myself. I thought, "Hmm...I've left him all these messages; he hasn't returned my call once. I don't know if this is such a good idea if I just walk in without an appointment." In other words, the fear had kicked in. Then I thought to myself: What's the worst-case scenario? The worst-case scenario is I walk in, and Dave says, "Eric, I'm not interested in having you speak to my team." Big deal—I could just walk out, get in my car, and return to my office.

Then I thought this: What's the best-case scenario? The best-case scenario would be that Dave books me to be a guest speaker. It became clear to me that, fear or not, I had nothing to lose by walking in announced, to try to meet with Dave. Worst-case scenario, I'm back in my car. When they announced me to Dave, he came out and said, "Eric Lofholm, you are one persistent son of a gun! Come back into my office." We went back to his office and we set the appointment. Remember:

You can follow up even if you're afraid.

I taught this mindset to one of my star clients, Mike Greaves of So-Cal Signs. A number of years ago while working with Mike I taught him the philosophy to follow up, follow up, follow up, until they buy or die. Mike found a very large account opportunity. A big sign for him would be around $5,000, and this sign would be for $20,000. The president of this company expressed interest in Mike doing the sign. So Mike followed up with him . . . but the president didn't call him back. Mike called again . . . still no reponse. Mike followed up with him again . . . well, you get the picture.

Now Mike has a dilemma—continue to call, or not? Not only that, he had two sales consultants giving him conflicting advice. I'm telling him to keep following up, while another sales consultant suggested that he move on to other prospects. Mike had to decide whom to listen to. He decided to listen to me, and continued to follow up with the president of the company. Eventually the deal closed, Mike did the job, and his company received a sale. Not only that, the president of the company was so happy with the job, he referred Mike to one of his friends and later Mike landed another big sign order, this one for $13,000. The moral of this story? This philosophy to follow up until they buy or die generated Mike $33,000 for his small business out of two sales.

This philosophy can also carry over into your personal life. Here's a funny story that I read about a few years ago. I was at the grocery store and was idly glancing at the tabloid magazines at the checkout stand. A *Cosmopolitan* magazine with Denise Richards—the famous model and actress who at one time was married to Charlie Sheen—caught my eye. According to the article, when the two first met, Sheen wouldn't call Richards for a date even though they seemed to really hit it off. She ended up pursing him. Now if a beautiful model and actress like Denise Richards has to follow up, you have to follow up, too!

Focus on Mindset

As we've discussed previously, mindset remains a critical component to each sales phase, particularly the idea of following up. Here are some negative mindsets about following up:

- I feel like I'm being a pest and bothering this person.
- If they were interested, they would call me back.
- What if they get mad at me for calling?

Here is the mindset of a sales champion regarding follow-up:

- I'm doing my job.
- I'm being a professional.
- I'm adding value.
- My job is to lead them to action.
- I'm a master of follow-up.
- I'm great at follow-up.
- They're still interested, it's just that life got in the way.

Say these Sales Champion mindsets to yourself over and over and over again to condition your mind to think like a sales champion.

I shared these powerful concepts with one of my clients, Kelly Goodman, and I taught her an idea that I'm going to share with you right now that made a tremendous difference for her on one of her sales calls. After giving your sales presentation and overcoming objectives (which I call dancing with the prospect), and they still want you to follow up later, understand that the prospect is most likely not in the sweet spot. The sweet spot is where you ask for the order. So when you follow up with the prospect, you need to get them back into the sweet spot. How do you do that? Let me share with you the technique I gave to Kelly. I told Kelly to begin by building trust and rapport with the prospect (even though you already met with them earlier), then say, "The last time that we spoke, you were very interested in working with me. Tell me, what interested you the most about us working together?"

Questions steer the focus of the conversation. By asking them this question, you help them re-focus on what previously interested them the most. I then told Kelly, after you get them interested again, simply say, "Since we spoke last, I thought of a story of a client that I've been working with that's just like you," and tell them a success story of someone you've been working with. At that point, you can then attempt to re-close, which means going through your entire close again.

The conversation might go something like this: "The last time we spoke, I shared with you information about this life insurance product (because Kelly sells life insurance), and I shared with you that the coverage you would receive is this, and the benefits are this, and the monthly investment that's required is this, and we'd start off and we'd have you do a medical exam. I can't promise that you're going to be approved, but if we are able to get you approved, we can then guarantee you the insurance at this monthly investment, and you'll have the option to move forward. Are you ready to move forward and take the next step to request the medical appointment?" (Or something along those lines.)

Later on, Kelly called me one time and said, "Eric! Eric! You'll never believe it, I used your follow-up technique and closed the sale!" I asked her how much commission she made on that single sale, and she said $11,000. What's exciting for Kelly is that she can use that follow-up technique over and over and over again for the rest of her career. And so can you.

Key Point

To help a prospect re-focus on the many benefits of working with you, ask them this question:

"The last time that we spoke, you were very interested in working with me. Tell me, what interested you the most about us working together?"

Ideas Into Action

Stay diligent in taking the sale to a conclusion of a "yes" or a "no"; *follow up, follow up, follow up until they buy or die.* That one single idea will pay for your investment in this book hundreds of times over.

Key Points Review

- You must make prospect follow-ups a key part of your sales success program.

- Don't be afraid to follow up; ask yourself, what's the worst thing that could possibly happen?

- Vary the ways you attempt to re-connect with prospects and clients.

- Remember my mantra: Follow up, follow up, follow up until they buy or die.

Chapter 12

Generating Unlimited Referrals

For most people, referrals are critical to their business success. Rate yourself on a scale of one to ten in the area of referrals. Do you have multiple people supplying you with referrals? Are the referrals you receive legitimate prospects, or more like tire-kickers? Do a significant percentage of your referrals turn into closed business deals?

Referrals are important because they not only generate immediate sales, but also sales which can happen over and over. In fact, a great referral exercise is to identify the financial value of a quality referral. Consider this question: How much is a quality referral worth to you financially? When you consider this, think of a concept called "lifetime value." In other words, you might have bought this book at a Barnes & Noble store, and I made $1. But let's say you really connected with my message, and became a client for life. The immediate sale was $1, but you might spend $10,000 with me over the lifetime of our relationship together.

If you don't ask for referrals, you are potentially leaving a huge amount of money on the table. So before you read on, take some time right now and really think through what is the lifetime value of a quality referral to you. If your answer is over $1,000, I want you to pay close attention to this chapter, and later read it over several times. Don't just gloss over it. If the value of a quality referral for you is over $1,000, the concepts in this one chapter alone could bring you an extra $100,000. There is one referral system that I'm going to teach you in this chapter that has generated over ten thousand referrals for me from one single idea. And this particular idea wasn't even mine; I learned it from someone else.

Referral Mindset

Before we dive too much into how to generate quality referrals, let's review that all-important topic: mindset. There's an Inner Game to referrals. Here are some common negative beliefs about referrals:

- I feel like I'm bothering the person when I ask for referrals.
- I'm not good at referrals.
- It's hard to get referrals.

Here are some positive referral beliefs:

- People love to give me referrals.
- It is easy to get referrals.
- I am a referral master—each day, I'm getting better and better in the area of referrals.

Say those positive referral affirmations to yourself over and over and over again until they have become part of your referral mindset.

Referral Tips

It's important to understand why people give referrals to others. Here are several common reasons:

- They simply want to help you.
- You asked for referrals.
- They want to help the person that they are referring (the prospect).
- They are motivated to give a referral.

Study the referrals you receive. Which of the above categories do most of your referrals fall into? Is this good or bad? Is there something you could do to make a slight adjustment to any of the above, to begin receiving more referrals?

Referral goals also play a key role in your sales success. Goals act like magnets—they attract to you what your goals are. Most people don't have referral goals. I've done live seminars where I've declared a goal of generating a thousand referrals in the seminar. On numerous occasions, we've exceeded a thousand referrals in a single seminar.

I also believe it's vitally important to develop *referral systems*, an organized or systematic approach to generating referrals. Many companies have affiliate programs. One of my referral systems is my affiliate program. In my affiliate program, I have a formal financial relationship with someone providing me referrals. For example, if you have an interest in earning income from referring business to me, you can become one of my affiliates. Go to

http://www.saleschampion.com/eric-lofholm/sales-training-programs/affiliates/

for details. It only takes a minute. Once you register as an affiliate, you can refer me business and earn income. In fact, you can earn back your investment in this book by providing a single referral.

Here's another tip: attempt to build as many reciprocal referral relationship as possible. In other words, identify other people who have your target market in their network. Let me give you an example. Say you are a real estate agent. A good reciprocal referral relationship would be someone in the financial services field, particularly mortgage lending. Let's say that you met someone in the mortgage business and spent some time getting to know and trust them. Now the two of you make an agreement: You refer your clients needing a mortgage to this person, and they refer their clients needing a real estate agent to you. Reciprocal in this case means that you both benefit.

What's neat about this concept is that you could create a reciprocal relationship with ten or more other professionals just like you. Again, let's say you are a real estate agent—your reciprocal relationships could include a mortgage professional, a tax preparer, a Certified Public Accountant (CPA), and so on. Perhaps you are a marketing consulting. You could form reciprocal agreements with someone who creates web sites, a printer, a graphic designer, and a photographer. The list can go on and on. By creating these relationships, it's like having ten salespeople out there promoting your business . . . without costing you a dime! Can you say "free marketing"?

Exercise

Think about whom you could, over time, approach to develop reciprocal relationships. Brainstorm now about the various industries and businesses these professionals might be part of:

1. _____

2. _____

3. _____

4. _____

5. _____

6. _____

7. _____

8. _____

9. _____

10. _____

11. _____

12. _____

13. _____

14. _____

15. _____

Another way to build ongoing, solid referrals is to create a referral script. Many people say to me, "Eric, I ask for referrals and I never get them." I always respond, "Congratulations, you've figured out a script on how to **not** get referrals!" Human beings respond in predictable ways. Once you find something that works, simply do it over and over and over again.

Another way to receive referrals is to give something in return. Let me give you an example I have used to generate more than ten thousand referrals. Years ago, I was a trainer for Tony Robbins, and when I trained for him, I would go in to companies and deliver a thirty-forty minute presentation to sell his seminar tickets. One day I was watching a video of a former Tony Robbins trainer named Wajed Salam. In the video, Waj handed out a referral form and said to the audience, "If you can help me out today with three or more referrals of other companies that I could contact about being a guest speaker, then I will reward you with a Tony Robbins audio cassette." I went to my manager and said, "I was watching this video of Waj Salam, and he implemented this referral strategy system, and I think it's a good idea. Do you think I should do it?"

My manager said, "No, you should just have one focus in the presentation—selling tickets. If you ask for referrals, you'll have two focuses."

Well, thank goodness I didn't listen to my manager, because I started implementing that idea and began to consistently receive an average of ten referrals per appointment. By doing two appointments a day, I begin receiving twenty referrals a day—or more than 400 per month. Nice!

Fast-forward a bunch of years. After I left the Tony Robbins organization to start my own sales training company, I continued to make presentations, except instead of promoting Tony's seminars, I was promoting my own. And when I promoted my own seminars, I offered a free Eric Lofholm audio CD in exchange for three referrals. Later still, when I had built a sales team, they would go out and offer a free Eric Lofholm CD in exchange for three or more referrals. All in all, I've used this strategy to generate more than 10,000 referrals. Nice, huh?

Here's a variation on what I just mentioned. Sometimes when I teach seminars, we'll do a variation of the strategy—instead of offering a free audio CD, I'll offer a free report in a portable document format (PDF) on Sales Scripting, or on the Sales Mountain. What's neat about providing the free report is that I can send the PDF out without it costing me anything, yet the client still receives something of value (the information in the report).

When I teach my live seminars, we'll often turn the referral-giving process into a contest. For example, I'll reward whoever provides the most referrals with one of my Level 10 pins. Let me share a secret—that pin only costs a little over a buck. I recently did a seminar with Robert Imbriale, one of my mentors and good friends, in attendance (his website is **www.ultimatewealth.com**). Robert watched me share this idea of asking for referrals and offering a free PDF report in exchange for helping me with referrals, with the winner receiving a Level 10 pin. And Robert thought it was hysterical that I was able to get roughly 500 referrals that day…all in exchange for a $1.25 pin. Plus, everyone had fun with the contest. How cool is that?

Ask and You Shall Receive

Here's another referral system I've used to generate more than 10,000 referrals—Ask, Educate, Easy, Incentive. Of course you must first ask for referrals. The key, of course, is to ask in the right way.

To help people give you great referrals, you must educate them on what a good referral is. For example, I say to my clients something like this: "A good referral for me is a sales manager or network marketing leader who has six or more people working for him or her anywhere in the world." Notice how specific I make this.

What makes a good referral for you? Consider these characteristics of your previous or current clients:

- Where you have worked in the past
- Where your clients work
- Industries where you have worked in the past
- The types of industries that would benefit from your products or services

To take this a step further, I would then say: "If you could help me out today with three or more referrals, I'll reward you by giving you a free audio CD." And so I would educate the client on what a good referral is.

To make the referral-giving process easy, I hand out a "fill in the blanks" form for people to write down their referrals. It can't get much easier than that, right? Remember, the easier you make it for people to provide you with referrals, the more referrals you'll receive.

Finally, there's incentive. Again, I usually offer a free Eric Lofholm CD in exchange for the referrals.

Implementing this Ask-Educate-Easy-Incentive system, and then just doing it over and over and over again, has generated more than 10,000 referrals.

Follow Your Money

One of my star clients, Doak Belt, has developed a lead generation system he calls Follow Your Money. In this system, Doak focuses on asking for referrals from people he is or has been a client to (i.e., paid them money). He did this with me, and it was brilliant. First, he became a client of mine, and we moved from trust and rapport to developing a bond. Then one day Doak contacted me and asked to set up a telephone appointment with me to help give him referrals. I said sure.

He called me at the agreed upon time, and said, "Eric, are you in front of your database?" I said yes, and Doak said "Well, here's what a good referral is for me—it's someone who makes more than $100,000 a year, is a small business owner, who is married with kids and owns a home, and who you think I would enjoy working with. Of the people in your database, who would be the best referral for me?" I looked through my database, found a good match, and gave him the person's name and phone number. Doak then asked for their mailing address. When I asked why he wanted the mailing address, he said, "I am going to send them a letter letting them know you referred me to them, and to be expecting my phone call." When I asked him why he did that, he replied, "Well, about half the time, the person receiving the letter will contact the person that referred them and ask about me."

Sure enough, of the three people that I referred Doak to, one of those three contacted me and asked me about Doak. Best of all, Doak ended up doing business with that individual. Does it end there? No! Doak has set up referral appointments with me on numerous occasions. He can come back to me two, three, four times a year for life and set up these referral appointments, because I am a big believer in him and I am willing to support him at that level. Think about this in your business—how can you find "raving fans" of yours that you can go back to over and over and over again, asking for referrals?

Exercise

1. Do you have any "raving fans"? Who are they: _____

_____

2. What steps can you take today to begin developing one or more raving fans? _____

_____

Ideas Into Action

Please take a moment now to reflect on the original idea of this chapter—what's the financial value, the lifetime value, of one quality referral? Remember that when you ask for referrals, you're creating that possibility of receiving that income in the future, and when you don't ask for referrals, you're leaving that amount of money on the table. You want to develop multiple referral systems and do them over and over and over again. This is critical to you making more sales, and it's very possible that the implementation of the ideas in this one chapter will generate more than $100,000 for you. They've generated far more than that for me.

Key Points Review

- Referrals are critical to your business success.

- Realize that referrals have a lifetime value that is far greater than just one immediate sale.

- Develop a positive referral mindset.

- Develop one or more referral systems.

- Develop at least one reciprocal referral relationship.

- Remember, to receive referrals, you must ask for them!

Chapter 13

Sales Scripting

In my seventeen-year journey studying sales I have learned over 1,000 sales ideas. I am a collector of great ideas. I have become a walking encyclopedia when it comes to sales ideas. Sales scripting, hands down, is the most profitable idea I have ever learned. I use prepared scripts during every main sales presentation I deliver.

If you're like many people, you're interested in how you can benefit from sales scripts…even though you also might be a little unsure exactly what scripting is. You don't want to sound canned or rehearsed, which some sales scripts come across as.

I want to take a moment now to acknowledge you not only for reading *The System*, but also to being open-minded about exploring how scripting can help you. One of my favorite quotes goes like this:

> *There is nothing more powerful than a good idea whose time has come.*
> —*Victor Hugo*

Right now may be the perfect time for you; *you* may be in the right place at the right time to learn, absorb, and use this information on scripting to help elevate you to that next level of success.

Sales Scripts: A Definition

In my public seminars, I often ask the audience, "By a show of hands, how many of you use sales scripts?" Usually, less than 50 percent of the audience says yes. Then I ask, "By a show of hands, how many of you don't use sales scripts?" The rest of the audience, which is usually more than 50 percent, raise their hands. Here's what I tell them:

> *The reality is, whether you think you're using scripts or not,* you are using scripts.

Now you might be saying to yourself right now, "Eric, you don't know what you're talking about. I don't use sales scripts." Yes, you do, and I will share with you why shortly. For now, here's an interesting question: Why do people resist scripting? Most people respond by saying they don't want to sound canned, rehearsed, inauthentic, robotic, they don't feel that scripts are flexible, and so on. If that were *my* view of what scripting is, then I wouldn't want to use scripts either.

However, what if that's not what scripting is? What if scripting is something *totally* different? What if scripting made you more powerful, more persuasive, and helped you and your client at the same time? Would you want to learn more about it? Its power? How it can transform you into a persuasion master? If this speaks to you, then you are reading the right material, at the right time.

Let me state this again: In reality, we *all* use sales scripts. You're either using a script or you're speaking in gibberish. Gibberish is *word salad,* or random words.

Of course, you don't speak in gibberish. Let me give you an example. Suppose that I asked you to deliver a presentation today, one that you've never delivered before. You would probably get the details from me, then deliver the best presentation possible. The second time you delivered this presentation, you would repeat much of what you said the first time. The *third* time you delivered this presentation, a lot of what you said the first and second times you'd say again. In other words, you would have effectively *drifted* into a script. People think, *Oh, I don't use scripts because I don't want to be scripted!* In reality, however, you *are* scripted; it's just that you drifted into a script.

If you accept the fact that you use scripts, the key question then becomes this: How *effective* are your scripts? You have two choices. You can either continue to wing it, creating your scripts by drifting into them. Or, you can prepare powerful, persuasive scripts that will make you more confident, more consistent, and add more value to your clients, all of which will bring you more business day after day, presentation after presentation, for the rest of your career. If you're ready to use sales scripting to make more sales, sign your name here:

❏ **Yes! I plan to use sales scripting in all my presentations and key interactions.**

Signed: _____

Date: _____

Earlier I said that scripting is not canned. It's not rehearsed. It's not inauthentic. It's not robotic. But it *is* flexible. So what is scripting?

A script is a series of words in sequence that have meaning.

Scripts absolutely are flexible. They are powerful. They are prepared. They are persuasive. Simply put, sales scripting is the most *powerful* way for you to improve your presentation results. Wow, pretty important, right? Let me repeat that . . . seven times.

Sales scripting is the most powerful way for you to improve your presentation results.

Sales scripting is the most powerful way for you to improve your presentation results.

Sales scripting is the most powerful way for you to improve your presentation results.

Sales scripting is the most powerful way for you to improve your presentation results.

Sales scripting is the most powerful way for you to improve your presentation results.

Sales scripting is the most powerful way for you to improve your presentation results.

Sales scripting is the most powerful way for you to improve your presentation results.

Consider this example: When a world leader like former British Prime Minister Tony Blair makes a speech, do you think that he makes up that speech as he goes along? Or do you think he's using a prepared script? **You see, when everything counts, people use a prepared script.**

Imagine that you were the owner of an organization that has fifty sales people. Would you want them using *persuasive* scripts, or would you want them making up their presentations on the fly, so to speak? Of course you would want them using persuasive scripts.

Here's a quick story to illustrate this point. Years ago, my first sales job involved selling over the telephone. I had no background in sales. On my first day on the job, my manager didn't give me any training. He just handed me a stack of leads and said, "Eric, go sell." As you can imagine, I performed poorly. In fact, I was the bottom producer at that company the first year that I worked there. No scripts. No training. Just go make it happen.

At the end of my first year, I missed quota two months in a row, so my manager, Richard Hogan, pulled me into the office. "Eric," he said, "Selling isn't for everybody, and apparently it's probably not for you. Either meet your quota this next month or you're out!"

My back was against the wall. At this point I was newly married. I was so embarrassed by being on quota probation that I didn't even tell Jarris. I just hoped and prayed that I would hit quota, which was $10,000 a month in gross sales.

But then something special happened. The top producer in the company, Tony Martinez, hired me to be his field assistant. I would continue to work for Dante Perano during the week and I would travel with Tony and help him on the weekends. Each weekend I would get one-on-one time with Tony. Tony started teaching me about scripting. Tony's coach was Dr. Donald Moine. Dr. Moine taught Tony about Scripting. Tony started teaching me what he had learned from Dr. Moine. I took those techniques and began *applying* them to my career.

What happened? As I believe you know (!), that next month, on quota probation, I generated $10,500 in gross sales. I made quota by literally *one sale*. I was *that close* to getting fired.

Anthony Gonya was on the sales team with me (we sat next to each other). He was on quota probation, too. He did $9,500 in gross sales . . . and was fired the next day.

The next month, with this scripting information, I generated $51,000 in gross sales. Seven months later, I generated $160,000 in a single month! How did I create these *powerful* sales breakthroughs? Sales scripting—the most powerful way for you to increase your sales results.

Sales scripting can help anyone. Later on, I began public speaking. A gentleman by the name of Ted was in the audience one day. At the time I was twenty-three. Ted, a best selling author and very successful businessman, was much older than me. I spoke to about forty people, and had a very successful sales result—I did $40,000 in sales using the scripting systems that I learned from Tony and Dr. Moine. Ted watched me speak, and afterwards he said, "Wow! This audience is just a buying audience!" The next day Ted gave his presentation to the same audience. He thought he was just going to do incredibly well. Instead, he closed *zero sales*. How did a young kid (me) outsell a best selling author $40,000 to zero? Sales scripts. I had a script that moved people to action and Ted did not.

A couple days later, Ted and I discussed what had happened. I said, "You know, there's a reason why you didn't close any sales."

He looked skeptical. "Well, why is that?"

"You teach a real estate *system*, right?"

"Yes."

"Well, there's a *system* for selling from the front of the room."

Ted was intrigued. "Do you know the system?"

"Sure. How else do you think I could sell $40,000 to forty people?"

Ted said eagerly, "Could you teach me the system?"

I smiled and said, "Yes, teaching is my gift."

So I taught Ted the system. The next time he spoke, he closed 20% of the audience on a $2,000 product. He went from zero to 20% in the snap of fingers, using the power of sales scripting. *Selling is a system*!

Why Sales Scripts Work

Why do scripts work? Simple: human beings respond in predictable ways. Let me give you an example. If you do what a millionaire does, you'll get what a millionaire has. If you invest your money where millionaires currently have their money invested, what will you become? If you were with me here today, you would say, "A millionaire."

Now, I've asked that question to literally thousands of people, and every person—*every person*—gives the same answer: a millionaire.

Prediction is a form of power

—Dr. Donald Moine

In your presentation, wouldn't you like to know what you're prospects are going to say *before* they say it? Well, that is the *power* of sales scripting.

I'm going to give you a million-dollar idea right now. It's your first scripting technique, and it goes like this: You can borrow other people's scripts. I didn't make up from scratch the script I just shared with you about the millionaire. I borrowed it from someone else. You can do the same—borrow other people's scripts.

If you're still not sure about the power of scripting, listen to what Michael Gerber, one of the world's leading experts on teaching business owners how to raise their level of success and the man behind the book *The E-Myth,* has to say about scripting. This is a direct quote from the book:

> *Things need to be sold and it's usually people who have to sell them. Everyone in business has heard of the old song 80 percent of our sales are produced by 20 percent of our people. Unfortunately few seem to know what the 20 percent are doing that the eighty percent aren't.*

The 20 percent use a system, unlike the other 80 percent!

Let's take this a step farther. Sales scripting is part of your *selling system*, a fully-orchestrated interaction between you and your customer. A selling system follows five primary steps:

Step 1:   Identification of the specific benchmarks or consumer decision points in your selling process.

Step 2:   The literal *scripting of the words* that will get you to each consumer decision point successfully. (Yes, written down, like the script for a play.)

Step 3:   The *creation* of various materials to be used with each script.

Step 4:   The memorization of each benchmarked script.

Step 5:   The *delivery* of each script by your salesperson in identical fashion.

If *you* put a sales system involving scripting to work in your company, you will see amazing results regardless of what kind of business you're in.

Now, here is your next scripting technique. It's called third-party endorsements. I just used this technique: instead of me telling you about the benefit of scripting, I allowed Michael Gerber to tell you about it. Michael Gerber, to me, is a third party. So instead of Eric Lofholm saying you should use scripting, now someone else makes that statement. That's a technique that you can use in your presentation, in *your* scripts. Instead of *you* saying a statement, appeal to a third party.

The *Wall Street Journal* says ... *Time* magazine says ... The local newspaper says ... This celebrity says ... This author says ... This is a very powerful scripting technique.

Types of Sales Scripts

Let's talk about script types. There are appointment-setting scripts, referral scripts, presentation scripts. If you sell on conference calls, there are conference-call scripts. There are hiring scripts, recruiting scripts, front-of-the-room scripts, objection handling scripts, closing scripts, and others as well.

Winning sales scripts contain a set of key *ingredients*. These ingredients are:

- The benefits of your product or service
- Probing questions (questions you ask the prospect to identify their needs)
- The offer (which comes at the end of the presentation, when you're explaining to the prospect what you're offering)
- The following go into the offer:
  - The price of your product or service
  - What's included
  - The length of the agreement
  - What the terms are
  - If there's a guarantee
  - What bonuses there are
  - What incentives there are

- Stories: look for stories that you can tell in your presentation; these could be your story, your company's story, and so forth
- A laundry list of the common objections

Scripts contain these *ingredients*. Now, I just used a scripting technique in teaching you the ingredients of a script, called *connect the known to the unknown*. This is one of my favorite techniques because part of selling is education. You see, you know your product and service far better than your prospect ever will. Part of selling is getting your prospect to understand the benefits like you understand the benefits. One of the ways to do this is to connect the *known* to the *unknown*. Think about your sales presentation. What are some of the things that you need to educate your client on to understand your product or service?

I want to give you a quick story, a real-world example of how somebody could use this technique in their sales presentation. This is a story about Ted Williams, the famous Boston Red Sox baseball player and the last player to bat over .400 for a season. You might also know that Williams, when he passed away, never received a proper burial. Instead, he was cryogenically frozen. His family had a huge squabble over this. It's really sad because one of the greatest American heroes of all time never received a proper burial.

That's a story that a lot of people are familiar with. I've thought about how somebody could use that story if they sold pre-need funeral arrangements. In the funeral business, there's pre-need, and there's at-need. Think about buying your funeral plot and casket. Pre-need is when you're still alive and you buy it. At-need means that you passed away without a burial plot or casket pre-bought, and now someone else in your family must make these decisions. There are salespeople who sell pre-need and are very successful at it. One of the objections that they get is this: *Why would I want to meet with you, Mr. or Ms. Pre-Need Salesman? I don't want to talk about death.*

The salesperson must create a compelling reason to meet with them. If I were selling pre-need, I would say something like this:

Eric: "Are you familiar with Ted Williams?"

Prospect: (Either says yes or no—it doesn't matter which.)

Eric: "Well, Ted Williams is one of the greatest American heroes of all time. He played for the Boston Red Sox. He was inducted into the Hall of Fame. Do you know what happened to Ted Williams after he passed away?"

Prospect: (Either says yes or no—it doesn't matter which.)

Eric: "Ted Williams was cryogenically frozen, and to this day has never received a proper burial. Let me ask you a question. If Ted Williams had the opportunity to get all these arrangements taken care of while he was still alive, if he could go back in time and get all this set up so that he could receive a proper burial, do you think that he'd want to receive that proper burial?"

Prospect: "Yes."

Eric: "That's why I do what I do, because when it comes time for somebody to need their funeral arrangements taken care of, this creates a tremendous amount of stress on the family. It can create a financial hardship. And, sometimes, the wishes of the person who passed are not carried out. What I like to do is help people get all of those arrangements taken care of and out of the way so your family doesn't have to worry about these details while going through the grieving process. I'd like to schedule an appointment to meet with you and your spouse to talk about your wishes when that time unfortunately comes."

Then I would set the appointment using the technique, *connect the known to the unknown.*

Again, I can almost hear you saying, "But Eric, I don't sell pre-need! What does this have to do with me?" You have challenges in your sales career just like the person who's trying to get their foot in the door with pre-need. You both can and should use sales scripting. This is a key idea. If I'm selling pre-need, I'm going to sell that same story time after time after time after time after time. It is going to open up opportunities to go on appointments I never would have obtained without that story.

Success Key: Preparation

I'm now going to give you another idea worth a thousand times the investment you have made in *The System*. It goes like this: Spend time preparing for each important sales call that you go on.

You will not always have the time to write down your scripts word-for-word. Prior to going on an important sales call, though, always be sure to review the following:

- The outcome you want for the presentation
- The benefits of your product or service
- The likely objections you'll receive, and your responses to these objections
- And lastly, the stories you will tell

Reviewing these essential items before your calls will boost your confidence and make your presentations go smoother, which will translate into a stronger delivery and a higher closing rate.

Exercise

First, make a list of all the scripts you'd like to create for your sales system:

_____   _____

_____   _____

_____   _____

_____   _____

_____   _____

Now prioritize this list by importance, with one being most important, and so on.

Look at your top three lists. Now I want you to imagine that those top three scripts are completed. What would the value be to you to have those scripts completed over the next twelve months? _____

Imagine how your life would be different if you were earning that additional income. Can you see your credit cards being paid off? Can you see yourself in your brand new dream car? Can you see yourself winning the sales awards in your company? How would that feel to be acknowledged in front of your peers and receive that sales award?

_____

_____

Now I want you to think about the value to you over the next ten years, because once the script's created, you're going to have a lifetime of benefit.

_____

_____

Finally, I want you to think about somebody you want to help in your life. By you making this additional income, how would you like to help them? Would you like to pay off their credit cards? Maybe it's your sister. Maybe it's your mom, and you went over to their house and you just gave them a check for $10,000 because she needed the money. Can you imagine how having the opportunity to give that kind of a gift to somebody would make you feel?

_____

_____

I hope you enjoyed that last exercise. Do you see a little better now the power of this information? This isn't just about writing some sales scripts and you making some more money. This is about changing your life so you can live the life of your dreams.

Scripting In Action

Let me break down some of the scripting techniques that I just used. The first technique is to establish a financial value on the scripts over the next twelve months. Do you offer a product or service where there is a future financial value to what you're offering? You see, once you take action and you create these scripts, there is an immediate benefit to you over these next twelve months.

If you went back and reviewed the exercise again, you'd also recognize I used the trigger-phrase, "imagine." When you use that phrase—*imagine*—it induces a trancelike state. It doesn't mean that somebody's going to buy from you, but it triggers something in their mind for them to *imagine* how their life would be different. When you're delivering an effective, high-quality sales presentation, your prospect is going in and out of a trance throughout the presentation. The word *imagine* can become a trigger-phrase to help your client visualize.

I then shared with you the benefit of the benefit. In other words, I talked about how once you have these scripts you can be more successful financially, but then I also said, "…and what would that mean to you? The new car, paying off your credit card debt? Doing something nice for a family member?" That has nothing to do with sales scripting. That has to do with the *benefit* of the scripting. The benefit of sales scripting is you make more money and you make more sales, but the benefit of *that* is that you pay off the credit card debt, or buy your dream car, and so on. People buy benefits.

The last technique I used was a future-pacing technique, where I took you into the future and got you *thinking* about delivering a $10,000 check to a loved one and how that would *feel*. I liken this to taking someone on a mental test drive, where they can experience—mentally—the benefits of your product or service. If you go to purchase a car, what do they want you to do? They want you to get in the car so you can *experience* the car. The smell. The sound. How the car drives. How it feels. Right? They want you to emotionally experience the car. When you are selling an intangible, like what I sell (sales training, or, in this case, sales scripting), you should take somebody on a mental test drive to get them to imagine the benefits.

These are all techniques that you could incorporate into your presentation.

Let's discuss one more scripting technique, called a direct command. Human beings respond to direct commands. Let me demonstrate this for you. Now that you're learning the importance of sales systems, a great next step for you with my company is to watch my videos on my sales systems. My videos are simply an audiovisual presentation of my training that you can view on your computer and mobile device. Here's the best part: The price is right because it's free! If you're enjoying this information in The System, you're going to love the videos.

How do you watch the videos? I'd like you to go right now to my website, www.saleschampion.com, and on the home page fill out the opt-in form. Enter your email address and you will be sent to a link allowing you to enjoy the videos right on your device immediately. The videos are free and available to everyone, so please let everyone know in your network who needs to learn about sales know about this great opportunity.

That was an example of a direct command. Here's another. I want you to create a Microsoft Word folder called "scripts" which will hold, from now on, all of your script work. You see, if you don't create that folder, you're going to have script work on scraps of paper and sticky notes and miscellaneous papers. I want all that information organized in one place.

Next, I'd like you to create a file for each script you want to create. You're going to name the file the name of the script that you want to create. For example, if you want to create a *referral* script, you're going to call the file "Referral Scripts" and then you're going to write out your referral script word-for-word.

Then I want you to create a sub-folder inside your main scripts folder called "Objections." You're going to make a list of the common objections in your industry (see Chapter 10 for review). Next, I want you to create a file within the Objections folder for each objection. Over time, you're going to develop ten to twenty responses to each of the common objections that come up.

Now, when I said ten to twenty responses, you might be thinking, "Eric, are you crazy? I don't know if I can come up with three or four responses!"

Come on—you're a professional! Over time, I want you to develop ten to twenty responses for each of the common objections that come up.

Planting Seeds

I have one more scripting technique to share with you. It's called a *seed sell*. A seed sell is where you plant the seed with your prospects. The idea is the seed, which, in time, will grow and eventually turn into a sale.

Would you like to learn how to become a master in the area of script writing? Once a year Dr. Donald Moine, my script-writing mentor and the top expert in the world in that discipline, and I teach a three-day boot camp in Las Vegas on script writing. It's the only script-writing program in the world. People fly in from all over the world to participate in our boot camps. To learn more about the next boot camp, go to my website or call my office.

Now, what I just did is a seed sell. I didn't give you a full sales pitch for Dr. Moine's boot camp. But I did let you know about the boot camp in a way that will get you subconsciously visualizing the possibility of attending it in the future and picturing the benefits of attending. This sows the seed of a possible sale. Of course a seed needs to be nurtured, and as in the Parable of the Sower, not all seeds grow to maturity. But for those of you open to the possibility of learning more from Dr. Moine, I've planted a seed that will grow as you are nurtured by the benefits you receive from this book and from staying in the conversation with me.

Ideas Into Action

As we wrap up let me share with you what we've covered in this learning system so far. You learned that you already use scripts even though you probably didn't realize it. You also learned some powerful scripting techniques. You are now ready to begin writing scripts.

To learn more, contact my office and find out how scripting can help you reach the next level of success. To really learn what I've shared with you about scripting, I want to strongly again encourage you to read this chapter again. How many times? That's right—seven times.

(What scripting technique did I just use? If you guessed direct command, you're right.)

Key Points Review

- A script is a series of words in sequence that have meaning.

- Whether you think you're using scripts or not, you are using scripts.

- Scripts are flexible, powerful, and prepared.

- Sales scripting is the most powerful way for you to improve your presentation results.

- Winning sales scripts contain a set of key ingredients: benefits, probing questions, etc. Know and use these key ingredients.

Chapter 14

GSA
(Goals, Strategy, Action)

This chapter contains one of the five best business-building ideas I know.

First, a little background. Remember how, about twenty years ago, I attended my first seminar, and there met Dante Perano, who would become my first mentor. That day Dante was sharing real estate investment strategies. During his presentation, he shared a story about an idea he had learned from J. Paul Getty's book, *How to Be Rich*. At one time, Getty was the wealthiest man in the world. Late in his career, he wrote this book about how he became successful. And according to Dante, Getty not only revealed his formula for wealth, he stated that if you applied this formula, you too could have anything that you want in your life.

When Dante shared that, I was skeptical. I had literally taken a day off of my job at McDonald's to attend this seminar. I was also a student in community college. At that point in my life, I had never achieved any level of success, so I was thinking, *Come on, how could one idea allow you to create whatever you wanted in your life?*

Although skeptical, I was still interested to hear what the formula was. It contained three letters: G-S-A, which stands for Goal, Strategies, and Action. Dante told us all that day, "All you need to do is ask yourself what do I want, then develop the strategy to achieve this, then take massive action on a daily basis."

I thought about that idea. Though still skeptical, a few months later I decided to try the idea out. I asked myself, "What do I want?"

The first thing that popped into my head was this: "Quit working at McDonald's."

So I made a decision and I quit. The second thing that popped into my head was that I no longer wanted to attend college. I had been attending college now for five years and had yet to complete two years' worth of college credits. College wasn't for me. I made a decision right then to quit school. The third thing that popped into my head was this: I wanted to communicate to the woman I was dating how much I cared for her. So what did I do? I went over and proposed to her on one knee at our favorite park in Rocklin, California, wearing my McDonald's uniform. (My wife told me years later, "I always knew I'd marry a man in uniform. I just didn't know it would be a McDonald's uniform." Speaking of Jarris, boy, did she take a leap of faith with me! I had quit my job, dropped out of school, and I didn't even have a ring for her, yet she still agreed to marry me. *Wow*—talk about the power of GSA!)

I made those three decisions in one single day. My life, and ultimately my destiny, changed after having made those three decisions. A decision without action is not a decision.

I've continued to think about this idea ever since Dante first told that story over twenty years ago. I've taught this concept to tens of thousands of people, and what has been true for me is this: The concept of GSA is one of the five best business building ideas that I have ever learned. In the remainder of this chapter, I am going to share with you how you can apply this idea to your business. Perhaps it will have a similar impact on you as it's had on me through all these years.

GSA: Goal - Strategy - Action.

The first part of GSA is Goals. Goal-setting is so important for sales success that I teach a whole ten-step goal setting system along with my sales system. I've included a bonus chapter later in this book teaching you all ten steps. You can read that chapter to learn my whole goal-setting system. In this chapter I just want to make one key point I emphasize there:

> *Write your goals down.*

This is one of the biggest keys to successful goal-setting, and it's so easy to do. All you need is a notebook and a few minutes. Read the bonus chapter for more about why this is so important and how to go about it for best results.

Now let's talk about Strategy and Action. In terms of elevating your results from where you are right now to where you want to go, which one do you think is more important: Strategy or Action? I have asked this question to more than a hundred audiences, and I always get a split answer. Which one do you think is more important?

I believe strategy is more important by a wide margin. Yes, we absolutely must take action. But most successes come after having taking the *right* action, not after having taken any action.

Consider this example. Starbucks has become one of the most dominant brands in the world. (I don't know if this will continue due to the current economic uncertainty and the price of their coffee, which some consider high. But right now, they are one of the dominant global brands.) When they started Starbucks, the owners had the vision to expand on a global level. Did the world need another coffee shop? Of course not. Did the world need a fancy coffee drink that cost $4 a cup? No. Yet Starbucks has been able to go out and dominate markets on a global basis. Is this because they slapped together a strategy and went out and took massive action? Or, did they develop a superior strategy, and only then went out and took the massive action? Of course, it was the latter—the superior strategy came first.

Starbucks used the POI strategy we discussed in Chapter 4 to help implement their global brand awareness. (POI, you remember, stands for Person of Influence.) Everyone in the world has a network. So do companies. Starbucks identified companies that had their target markets, then influenced these companies to serve Starbucks coffee. Ever been to an airport recently? There's a Starbucks there. When Starbucks influenced Barnes & Noble, they got access to more than five hundred Barnes & Noble stores.

Let me give you an example of how McDonald's used this concept to expand nationally. If you had a company and you wanted to expand nationally, you would probably face a cash flow challenge. In other words, how do you come up with the money needed to expand nationally? McDonald's, which wanted to expand across the nation (and later, the world), faced this challenge.

Let's look a little closer at a strategy. A strategy is like a completed puzzle. When you dissect a strategy, what you are left with are tactics. Tactics are like puzzle pieces. The strategy is the completed puzzle. Tactics woven together can form synergy. Synergy is doing more with less. Another way of describing synergy is: one plus one equals three. Sometimes one plus one equals thirty; sometimes one plus one equals three thousand; sometimes one plus one equals three million.

What I mean by this is that sometimes, when you combine tactics together—or companies together, or people together—something incredibly powerful happens. It's like when Ray Kroc met up with the McDonald brothers. Prior to meeting Kroc, the brothers had two successful McDonalds locations. When you blended Kroc with the burger concept that the McDonald brothers had come up with, it turned into a multi-billion dollar company. So when I say "one plus one equals three million," that's an example where Kroc, combined with the McDonald brothers, created something incredibly powerful.

McDonald's didn't have the money to expand nationally. To overcome this, they identified four different tactics. (I learned about this in the book *Grinding it Out*, written by Ray Kroc himself, telling the McDonald's story.) First, McDonald's bought land. Their second tactic was to build a structure. The third tactic was to brand the building a McDonald's. And finally, they would apply for, and secure, bank financing for operations.

Are any of these tactics individually very powerful or innovative? No. You could buy raw land; I could buy land. You could build a structure; I could build a structure. You could create a brand; I can create a brand. You could get bank financing for a piece of real estate, and I could as well. When you combine the tactics, though—when they bought raw land, built the structure, branded it, and obtained bank financing—the results were powerful. They found that the land and building cost about $150,000, yet after the McDonald's had been built, the land immediately appraised for $300,000. So they had a 50 percent loan to value ratio. (I don't know the exact numbers, but the ratio is accurate.) They then went to the banks and said, "We can show you that a built McDonald's is worth $300,000, and we only need a $150,000 loan to build one."

Needless to say, the banks lined up to give McDonald's money, and the rest, as they say, is history.

A Real Life Example

Tactics woven together can form synergy. Let me share with you now some real-world examples of clients of mine that have applied this principle. And then I want to give you an example of how I have applied this principle.

The first client is Joey Azsterbaum. He's in the loan business. When I met Joey, he was an average loan officer. He had had months where he earned $10,000 each month. But he also was what I call a Dow Jones salesperson—his results were up and down, and thus not predicable. I started working with Joey on his tactics. First, I encouraged Joey to get a database and begin a systematic direct mail program. (I always encouraged clients to keep contacts in a database. My database is one of my most valuable business assets.) Joey has two types of customers: retail loan customers, and also real estate agents who bring him their buyers.

So Joey created two groups within his main database—a realtor group and a consumer group. He then developed a direct mail strategy for each. Later, he added outbound telemarketing. Then he hired an assistant. Then he put up a billboard in town that stayed up for about a year. Then Joey hired a sales person. Now Joey also did other things, but these were the key ones. He wove those tactics together. Tactics woven together can form synergy. Since implementing these tactics, Joey has earned more than $30,000 *in a month*, and for the last two years has been named Loan Officer of the Year at his company. He is one of the best students that I have ever had at applying the concept of GSA in his business.

As shown by Joey, tactics can come in all shapes and sizes. You can increase fees. You can expand your product line or service offerings. You can do more marketing. What new tactics might you introduce in your business? Start thinking about how you can weave them together to work synergistically.

Let me share with you a way that I have applied this concept in my business. One of the ways that I help people is with sales scripting, and so I put up a one page website and the web address is:

www.freesalesscriptingreport.com

On this one page website, what's available is: a one-hour audio download, a word-for-word transcription (over fifteen pages) of that audio, and then there is a special report that reveals twenty-one different sales scripting techniques. The audio, the transcription, and the report are valued at over $100, and they are available for free at that website. You could go to that website right now and request those free tools.

So I put up that one page website and then when somebody goes to the website and requests the information, they enter their name, their phone number, and their email address, and that information automatically goes into my database. So that is a tactic.

And then we follow up with a phone call to the people that request the free report; that's a tactic. And the next thing we do is to develop the customer. The way we develop the customer is by offering them additional sales training products and services that would make sense for them.

So here is my projection of what's going to happen as a result of this strategy. Remember the strategy is the completed puzzle and the tactics are the puzzle pieces. The expected results from this website are 200 to 1000 leads per month at zero cost. That would generate around 5000 leads per year. From those 5000 leads I project that we would sell 500 DVDs at $49, 200 home study programs at $600, 100 boot camps at $1000 each, and twenty advance trainings at $5000 each. That would generate over $300,000 in revenue per year. In addition, those customers most likely will buy additional products and services in the future. We would also be generating referrals from those customers. Over the course of ten years this single idea is a $3-million idea—a great example of applied GSA.

Ideas Into Action

To apply the GSA strategy to your own business, I invite you to commit to three actions that will have a big impact on your results:

First, commit to writing down your goals. For tips on how to do this more effectively, study the chapter on goal-setting.

Second, commit to writing down your sales strategy. Write down the steps in your customized Sales Mountain as it applies to your business.

Third, commit to writing down your sales scripts, using the sales scripting techniques taught in Chapter 13. For more help with this, visit the website I mentioned earlier:

www.freesalesscriptingreport.com

Key Points Review

- The concept of GSA is based on billionaire J. Paul Getty's teaching that all you need to do to achieve anything in life is to ask yourself what you want, then develop the strategy to achieve it, then take massive action on a daily basis.

- For the Goal part of GSA, use the 10-step goal-setting system taught in the bonus chapter later in the book, and make sure to apply the key principle of writing your goals down.

- Strategy plays a bigger role in elevating your results than Action, so think about your strategy before taking action, and reflect on your strategy when your actions aren't getting the results you want.

- Taking action means applying tactics that turn your strategies into results.

- One of the best strategies you can put into action to achieve business results is writing down your sales scripts. You can get more help with your sales scripts by visiting:

www.freesalesscriptingreport.com

PART III

ACTION

Are you still with me? Good! Because the best is yet to come!

Up to now, we have laid the foundation for you to make more sales. In Part I, we covered the all-important Inner Game of Selling, which primarily has to do with your mindset and attitudes. In Part II, we dove into the critical nuts-and-bolts aspects of successful selling, from building trust and rapport to handling objections to sales scripting (and the key points in between!). While extremely valuable, the information and ideas contained in Parts 1 and 2 are worthless without Part III—taking action. It's not enough to know what to do; you must go out and do it, and you must do it over and over and over.

Here's the exciting news: I am completely confident that you have the ability to not only take action—to do the necessary sales elements, like building referral systems—but also that you have the ability to take action on a massive level. Why? Simply because I believe that, because you've read this material to this point, you're ready to make a dramatic positive difference in your sales career, and thus life.

Now I know that you might be panicking a bit, that fear might be creeping in, that the mountain peak of sales success looks so-o-o-o far away. Don't worry. To climb the mountain, you simply need to take one step at a time. The same is true with creating more sales.

Are you ready to take the actions necessary to dramatically change your life? Good! To begin, simply turn this page!

Chapter 15

Putting It All Together

Action is the number one key ingredient to all success and all achievement. With action anything is possible; without action, nothing is possible. One of my favorite quotes is this one:

> *The universe rewards people who take action differently than those who don't.*

Are you ready to take the necessary action to help you make more sales? Good, because in this chapter, I am going to show you how.

My Life-Changing Action Moment

Let me share a life-changing story about action with you now. It happened many years ago when I worked as a sales person for the Tony Robbins organization. Like most sales organizations, the company had various sales contests. For one contest, the winner would receive a weeklong, all-expenses-paid trip to Fiji. When Jarris and I eloped, not only were we young, we were broke, so we had never taken a honeymoon. So I saw this contest as a way to be a hero in my wife's eyes—win the trip, go on a belated (and free!) honeymoon.

There was more. In addition to the trip, Tony Robbins himself planned to attend. Needless to say, I was very pumped up to win this trip and set that as a goal, so I worked hard (took action). And guess what—I was fortunate enough to be one of the winners. Immediately I began to visualize the trip and what it was going to be like—the gorgeous tropical weather, the exotic food, spending time with my wife, and so on. Something else popped into my mind—at some point during that Fiji trip, I was sure that Tony himself was going to pull me aside, pat me on the back, and tell me what a great guy I was and how lucky he was that I worked for him. He was going to acknowledge me for the level of success I had achieved in my life to this point and acknowledge me as one of the contest winners.

So we go to Fiji, right? The week comes . . . and the week went, and never once did Tony Robbins pull me aside, pat me on the back, and tell me what a great guy I am. Now it's the last day of the trip and I'm disappointed that this hasn't happened. When I visualize something is going to happen, I *believe* that it's going to happen. (In fairness to Tony Robbins, of course, he knew nothing about my visualization.)

It came down to where there was thirty minutes left before the bus was going to take us to the plane to begin our return flights home. Right then, with thirty minutes left in the trip, I saw Tony Robbins having lunch by himself. Now in all the time that I had worked for Tony, I had never once seen him by himself. Tony thrives on people contact, and there are always—*always*—people around him. My brain immediately says, "Here's the opportunity I've been waiting for. I'll go over there and talk to Tony, and he'll acknowledge me, pat me on the back, and tell me what a great guy I am."

So I walk over to Tony and I say, "Tony, is it okay if I have a seat? I have some questions that I'd like to ask you." Now, I didn't have any questions that I wanted to ask him. I was just looking to get a pat on the back so I could have my visualization come true.

He says, "Sure Eric, have a seat." So I sit down. And he says, "What do you want to know?"

"Well, Tony, I am a young guy. I have some big hopes and big dreams of things that I want to do with my life. Do you have any advice for me?"

"Yeah, Eric. As a matter of fact I do."

"Great. What is it?"

He looked me square in the eye and gave me an answer totally different than what I was expecting. Instead of patting me on the back, he challenged me. To paraphrase a long answer, the gist I got out of what he said was, "In order for you to make your dreams happen, your actions need to be consistent with your goals.

And from what I've seen your actions are not consistent with your goals, so unless you take more action, you'll never make it." In essence, what Tony was saying amounted to, "Eric, either lower your goal or raise your level of action."

After giving what Tony said careful consideration, I realized that I would either need to raise my level of action or lower my goals. I decided to raise my level of action. As I applied this higher level of action to my sales activities with Tony Robbins, I rapidly became the top producer on my sales team. Over the next eight months, I outsold everyone on the team. And it wasn't because my sales skills had improved: it was because I was taking more consistent action.

The reason I want to share this story with you now is that I want you put yourself in a place where you are truly honest with yourself and ask yourself this critical, potentially life-changing question: Are your actions consistent with your goals and dreams?

Are they?

If you get the answer I got, my suggestion is that you do one of two things: either lower your goal or commit to taking more action. Either decision can be okay. If you truly can't follow through on the amount of action it would take to achieve the goal you've set, it's better to commit to a more realistic goal you can actually achieve.

But don't lower your goal without pushing yourself to try your best, either. You'd be surprised what you can achieve when you really commit to playing at a level 7 every day and playing at a level 10 as many days as possible. And you can renew your commitment every day when you wake up, or at any time during the day. Today is a brand new day. Literally, in this moment here and now, you can make a decision that you are going to get yourself to play at a higher level, that your actions will match your goals and dreams.

Whatever you decide, whether it's to lower your goal or to raise you action level, I want you to know that I believe in you. You have what it takes; you have greatness inside of you. I look forward to sharing your success story in one of my upcoming books, newsletters, or seminars. It's up to you to decide.

Stories About PLY

Why do I have such confidence that you can succeed beyond your wildest dreams? Simply because I've seen this over and over again with my clients. And these aren't "special" people, they don't possess anything you don't. I call these folks PLY: People Like You. Here are some PLY stories meant to boost your confidence and give you ideas.

David Laster

David Laster works for AFLAC. Several years ago he attended one of my seminars. At the time he was an average salesperson for AFLAC. He really connected with my message and my sales system, and in particular my belief to "stay in the conversation." David made a decision to stay in the conversation with me. Over the years he has attended many of my live events and also done frequent telephone coaching.

One idea in particular of mine that really made a big difference for David was to create a "Raving Fans" book, a book of testimonials from people singing your praises. David loved that idea. He felt it would help him in his presentations, and so he created his own Raving Fans book. He has testimonials and has been endorsed by more than 500 people. Last year, out of roughly 60,000 AFLAC reps nationwide, David ranked 45th. Pretty cool, huh? His great year won him an all-expenses-paid cruise in Monte Carlo. The following year, David won another free trip, this time to Maui. David has a nice twenty-thirty year career in front of him where he will make several million dollars in sales commissions. Way to go, David.

Wendy Phaneuf

I met Winnipeg, Canada, consultant Wendy Phaneuf on a conference call several years ago. She had just started her consulting business, and it was going so poorly that she was strongly considering getting a job with a company. She really connected with my message. She signed up for my Protégé program. She consistently plugged in on the weekly calls. In December of each year in the Protégé program, I teach you how to create your sales and marketing plan for the next year. When Wendy sent me her plan for 2005, I looked at it and told her that her goals were way too low. My intuition told me she was capable of making much more.

She readjusted her plan, increased her goal, and sent it back to me. It was still too low. Instead of giving her another opportunity, I emailed her back what I felt her goal needed to be. It was double her original goal.

Why so high? You see, I had started to believe in Wendy. I believed in her much more than she believed in herself. To her credit, she accepted my sales goal for her. In that year, 2005, Wendy nearly hit the number that I had emailed her. In 2006, she tripled her business. In 2007, she maintained that increase and at the same time took off the summer. That had been one of her side goals all along—to make enough money to take off the entire summer.

Wendy is now one of the top consultants in the world. Her website is **www.leadingforloyalty.com**. She helps managers and executive teams and employees all work well together to increase the results for the company. She transforms environments inside of companies. She is one of the best in the world at what she does. In the several years that I have worked with Wendy, she has improved her sales mindset, her sales scripting, and has taken massive action to achieve her goals.

Joey Aszterbaum

I met Joey Aszterbaum several years ago when I went to his company and did a free sales training. Joey then signed up for my Protégé program. At the time, he was an average loan officer. The best month he'd ever had was about $10,000 in income. But he wasn't consistent. Some months he'd do that well. Other months, though, he would hardly do anything. Within six months of working with me, Joey earned over $29,000 in a single month. Joey has gone on to become one of my best students. His website is **www.joeyloans.com**. Joey has become a master of time management, sales scripting, and taking action.

Arvee Robinson

Arvee Robinson is another one of my star students. I met Arvee in a seminar many years ago. At the time she was struggling in her business. She was uncomfortable selling and uncomfortable with sales scripting. She really connected with my message, however, of teaching people how to sell from honesty, integrity, and compassion. Arvee signed up for my program and I started to work with her. Arvee responded very well to my material and made a conscious decision to embrace sales, embrace sales scripting, and take massive action.

Arvee's income had gone from about $4,000 a month, to where she now regularly earns $15–20,000 a month. My vision for Arvee is that one day she'll earn over $100,000 in a single month. Arvee is a fantastic public speaking trainer and she has my full endorsement. If you are looking to grow your business giving speeches, go to **www.instantprospeaker.com** to see how Arvee Robinson can help you.

J'en El

I met J'en El, another one of my star students, only four months ago when she attended one of my seminars and really connected with my message. At that time she was already a top earner with USANA, and she had reached the Ruby level, which is an outstanding level in the company. However, when I met her, J'en El described herself as being in the Ruby Rut; she had been a Ruby for twelve years.

I helped J'en El access an even higher level of greatness inside of her, and I encouraged her to go for higher goals. Within four months of meeting me, J'en El became a Diamond with USANA. Attending my seminar was the catalyst for achieving those results. A few months later, she became part of the Million Dollar Club. She also won a free trip to Ireland as a result of being in the Top Growth 25 of the entire company, and then went on to win a free Mediterranean cruise to France, Spain, and Italy.

Mark Spahn

Mark Spahn is a business owner with his own lighting company. When I met Mark, his company was doing around $2 million per year. It allowed him to earn a nice income; not a great income, but a nice income.

Mark really connected with my message, took a couple of ideas and put them into "action," and as a direct result more than doubled his business. Specifically he applied the baseline strategy combined with goal setting. Recently, Mark closed escrow on his dream home. Mark is an amazing human being, and I'm so happy about the success I have helped him achieve.

Sigal Zoldan

Sigal is another one of my star students. Sigal specializes in training people to use their subconscious mind to create greater results in their business. When I met her, she possessed so-so sales skills. She really connected with my message, however, and attended one of my script writing trainings. She learned how to write scripts, and as a direct result has become outstanding in her sales skills. Sigal has increased her goal to make $20,000 a month. Recently she had her best day ever, closing more than $2,100 in her one-on-one practice in a single day.

Ideas Into Action

Remember, action is the number one key ingredient to all success and all achievement. Only by taking action on solid sales fundamentals (you still must take action on the right things to do) will you achieve massive results. Remember:

> *The universe rewards people who take action differently than those who don't.*

To start taking action on what you've learned from this book, go to the Success Journal at the end of the book where you've been recording the best ideas you've been learning as you've been reading. (Remember I told you to do that back in the Introduction?) Pick the two best ideas you've learned and focus on putting those into action first.

After you've made some progress implementing those ideas, pick another one to work on. Treat this as a workbook to study and apply, not just something you read once. The value you get out of this book will depend on what you put into applying it. I can teach you everything I know about sales, but it's up to you to take action. I encourage you to read this book at least seven times to really absorb the ideas in it on a deeper level. This is part of staying in the conversation.

I'd like to conclude by acknowledging you for finishing this book and offering you an opportunity to receive a certificate of completion as a reward. Completing tasks is what winners do. Pat yourself on the back for reading this far. (Don't worry, no one can see you!) Then email me at wins@ericlofholm.com, put "Finished Your Book" in the subject line, and tell me the two best ideas you got out of this book that you decided to put into action. I'll send you a certificate signed by me acknowledging you for completing this book. I want to hear your success story!

Key Points Review

- Action is the number one key ingredient to all success and all achievement.

- The universe rewards people who take action differently than those who don't.

- Why do I believe in you? Because I have literally helped thousands of PLY—People Like You—succeed beyond their wildest dreams.

- To receive your certificate of completion for finishing this book, take action on the two best ideas from your Success Journal and sending me an email telling me what ideas you picked with the subject line "Finished Your Book"s at:

    wins@ericlofholm.com

Part IV

Bonus Material

Bonus Chapter #1

Goal Setting Mastery

Goal setting is perhaps the most widely endorsed personal development idea in the world. Consider the following people who endorse goal setting: Oprah Winfrey, Michael Jordan, Pat Summitt (head coach of the Tennessee Lady Volunteers basketball team), baseball great Mark McGwire, Zig Ziglar, Napoleon Hill (a pioneer in the field of personal success literature), and actor Jim Carrey.

While important to success, goal setting is also one of the most misunderstood personal development ideas. Let me give you an example. Recently I attended a personal development seminar. The speaker asked each of us to write down on a sheet of paper ten of our goals in three minutes. At the end of the three minutes, I was surprised to find that I only had seven goals. The speaker then asked the group how many had ten goals. Of 1,000 people in the audience, only about fifty hands went up—or 5 percent of the audience.

The speaker said, "For a goal to be a goal, it must be written down. Most people think that goal setting is merely deciding what you want. That is only the first step. Goal setting is a *process*. If you are not following the process, then what you are doing is not goal setting." He went on to teach us his process. I was fascinated, because all along I thought I was goal setting, and I realized in that moment that I wasn't.

Since that day, I have been working on creating my own goal-setting process. I quickly looked for all for the goal-setting information I could find in books, on audio tapes, and on videos. From this study I have created my own goal-setting process. I believe it's the most powerful goal-setting process in the world. It's a ten-step process that will help you create the life of your dreams.

Why Don't People Set Goals?

Before we dive into my goal-setting program, let's study why people don't set goals. I believe that there are nine primary reasons people don't set goals:

Nine Reasons People Don't Set Goals

1. They don't know the importance of goal setting.
2. They don't know how.
3. They think they are already doing it.
4. They don't have any goals.
5. They are afraid of failure. By not setting a goal, there is no way to fail.
6. They don't believe in themselves. Achieving a goal is not a possibility in their minds.
7. They suffer from the curse of early success.
8. They are in a comfort zone.
9. They are afraid of success.

Let's look at each of these reasons a little more.

1. They don't know the importance of goal setting.

Can you become a millionaire without setting a goal of being a millionaire? Sure. Maybe you just inherited a million dollars. Perhaps you won the lottery. What are the chances, though, that you will either inherit a million dollars or win the lottery? Not very high. The chances of your becoming a millionaire without making it a goal are very slim. Thus, goal setting becomes important because by setting goals, you dramatically increase the chances of your getting out of life everything that you want. That's the main benefit of goal setting: to help you get anything you want in life faster and easier than without goals. Once people realize how important goal setting is, they immediately become goal setters.

2. They don't know how.

Where did you learn how to set goals? How effective was the teacher, the book, or the tape at teaching you the fundamental principles of goal setting? Most people have never been taught proper goal-setting techniques. A simple analogy to illustrate this point is a person who doesn't ski. The number one reason people don't ski is that they don't know how. Many people don't set goals because they don't know how.

3. They think they are already doing it.

Many people think they are already setting goals. In fact, you may be one of those people. You might have gone through your life until now believing that you were using proper goal-setting techniques. Consider the following example: a high school student might set the goal to have a GPA of 3.5. This is a fairly gifted student who, if he truly applied himself, could have a 4.0 GPA. At the beginning of the semester, his parents asked him what his GPA goal was for the semester. He responded with "3.5." His parents were satisfied with the answer and moved on to the next topic. That's not goal setting. The student achieved a 3.0 GPA. There is nothing wrong with a B average. But he had the academic ability to achieve a 4.0 GPA. He could have stretched his original goal, if had he followed proper goal-setting techniques.

4. They don't have any goals.

During the past ten years, I have met several people who tell me they don't have any goals. This isn't really true, though. They do have goals; they just have never taken the time to think about what they really want in life. Whenever I meet someone who says that they don't have any goals, and I ask them if they would you like to retire financially independent, what do you think they say? Of course, they say yes. Everyone has goals. Yet not everyone has taken the time to really think about what they want most in life, then write it down, then create a plan for achievement, and then, finally, take action.

5. They are afraid of failure.

Have you ever met someone who enjoys failing? I sure haven't. We all want to succeed in life. Many people are so afraid of failing that they don't try. They have the goal, the vision, and the dream in their minds, but they never take action because the thought of failure dominates their thinking and paralyzes their action. If you fall into this category, I suggest that you begin by setting small goals using proper goal-setting techniques. Once your confidence climbs, then move on to bigger goals.

Also, keep in mind that everything has a risk attached. Your goals have risk. (What if I fail?) There is also risk in not going after your goals. (What if I get through my life without going after what was most important to me?) For me, I would rather pursue my dream and fail than go through life asking, "What if?"

6. They don't believe in themselves.

If you don't believe that you have the talent to write a book, would you set such a lofty goal for yourself? Probably not. Our beliefs shape our behavior. In most cases, we will only attempt what we believe we can achieve. For some people this fact limits their experience. Every time they think of a compelling goal that excites them, they quickly tell themselves, "I could never do that." Yes, you can do that, and much more. Goal setting is not a belief exercise. I will say it again: *Goal setting is not a belief exercise.* Goal setting is an exercise in clearly defining what you want, writing it down, creating a plan for achievement, and taking action.

7. They suffer from the curse of early success.

Some people achieve success at an early age. They try different things and success comes easily to them. Later, though, life deals them some sort of blow—as life tends to do. All of a sudden, success doesn't come so easily. In fact, they begin to fail. They lose their company. They go bankrupt. They get divorced. They lose that unstoppable confidence they had, and they stop setting goals. What goals have you given up? When do you tell yourself you are too old, not smart enough, not talented enough, don't have enough time, don't have enough money? Whatever reason you have for not succeeding, I can show you someone who has faced greater adversity and succeeded.

8. They are in a comfort zone.

Many people live their lives as comfortably as possible. They have no desire to strive for more out of life. I accept that answer. There is nothing that says we need to constantly be striving for more. However, I have one question for a person who is in the comfort zone. Do you truly have what you want out of life, or are you settling for less?

9. They are afraid of success.

What if you had a big goal, such as becoming CEO of a Fortune 500 company? This goal appeals to you because you would be the boss. You would make an extraordinary income. But then you start thinking, "What if I do become a CEO? What about all of that responsibility? What about all that stress?" All of a sudden, you begin to fear the consequences of success. Consider this question:

If a person fears what will happen if he succeeds, how likely will he get started? Not very. Do you have goals you aren't pursuing because you fear the consequences if you succeed?

The Power of Written Goals

Why should I set goals and write them down? Goal setting is not goal setting unless the goal is written down. Here are nine reasons you should set goals and write them down:

Nine Reasons You Should Set Goals and Write Them Down

1. Written goals help you reduce stress by creating a compelling future for you.
2. Written goals point you in the direction you want to take.
3. Written goals activate your subconscious mind.
4. Written goals help you clearly communicate your life plans to others.
5. Written goals increase the likelihood that you will accomplish your goals by 1,000%.
6. Written goals improve your time management skills.
7. Written goals motivate you.
8. Written goals help you manage the coincidences in your life.
9. Written goals help you create the life of your dreams.

Let's look at each in more detail.

1. Written goals help you reduce stress by creating a compelling future for you.

What causes stress? I have often thought about that question. I believe fear of the future causes stress. If you had no fear of the future, would you have stress? My answer is no. Written goals help you reduce stress by creating a compelling future for you. If you are excited about the future and what it holds for you, will that reduce any fears that you might have about the future? The answer, of course, is yes. In contrast, if you approach the future with fear and worry, will you probably feel stress about the future? Of course, you will. Written goals will help you reduce stress by creating a compelling future for you.

2. Written goals point you in the direction you want to take.

What would happen if you got in a boat in San Francisco and you had no idea where the boat was going? Where would you end up? The right answer is wherever the boat was going. Now what if you went to the San Francisco pier and saw three boats there: one was a luxury liner headed for Alaska, the second a fishing boat headed for Japan, and the last one a private yacht headed for Los Angeles. You can board any of the three boats. Your goal is to get to Japan. Which boat would you board? Of course, you would pick boat two, the fishing boat headed to Japan. Now consider this: The fishing boat is the least luxurious of the three, and has the longest ride. In spite of these factors, you should still take the fishing boat because it would help you reach your destination. Written goals point you in the direction you want to take.

3. Written goals activate your subconscious mind.

Have you ever gone to bed and, right before you fell asleep, you were thinking about a problem in your life, then in the middle of the night you awoke with the answer? That is your subconscious mind working for you. Another example is when the server asks you for your drink order at a restaurant. Do you find yourself telling the server what you want to drink without thinking about it? This is an example of your subconscious mind working. An iceberg is a great metaphor for the power of your subconscious mind. When you are on the surface of the water, you can see the tip of the iceberg—your conscious mind. Beneath the water, though, you will see a much larger mass of ice—your subconscious mind. Your subconscious mind has a tremendous influence on your behavior. I don't really understand how it works. I just know that it *does* work. Written goals activate your subconscious mind.

4. Written goals help you clearly communicate your life plans to others.

Many of your goals will require the assistance and cooperation of others. One skill you will need to develop is the ability to clearly communicate your goals to others. When you go through the process of writing down your goals, you improve this ability to communicate your goals to yourself. Once you have clearly communicated your goals to yourself, you will automatically improve your ability to communicate your goals to others.

5. Written goals increase the likelihood that you will accomplish your goals by 1,000%.

A great example for this (which many people can relate to) is a wedding. When you planned your wedding, did you write down your goals? Chances are you did. And do you believe that effort increased the probability that your wedding plans would be realized? Without the written goals, the overall plan for the wedding would have been lost. Written goals increase the likelihood that you will accomplish your goals by 1,000%.

6. Written goals improve your time management skills.

Goals give your life direction. When you have direction, you know where to focus your time and energy. If your goal is to become the top real estate agent in your area, should you take a job as a receptionist? No, of course not. You would do your best to land a job as a real estate agent. My point is that many people have jobs that are not helping them achieve their dreams, because they have never taken the time to think about what they want and write it down. Written goals give a clear idea of the best ways you can invest your time.

7. Written goals motivate you.

I am a sales coach. I have met thousands of salespeople who hate to make cold calls. On a scale of one to ten, their motivation to make sales calls is one. I have also met many salespeople who are extremely motivated to make cold calls. What is the difference between the two? I have found that the motivated salespeople focus on the *benefits* they are receiving by making the cold calls. In other words, they have invested time to clearly communicate to themselves the specific benefits they are receiving by making the calls. When you have written goals, you have a plan in writing that communicates to you the benefits you are going to receive once you take action. Written goals motivate you.

8. Written goals help you manage the coincidences in your life.

Have you ever had a goal that manifested itself by coincidence? Here is an example that happened to my wife and me. When we moved into our house, we wanted to get a new kitchen table. Within thirty days of writing down that goal, our friend Mark offered us a brand new kitchen table with four matching chairs for free. The table, had we bought it new, would have cost over $1,000. Events like this happen every day. When I am very clear regarding what I want and follow the ten-step goal-setting process (which I'm about to share with you!), I find that coincidences like that happen all the time. Test it out. Become clear about what you want, follow the ten-step goal-setting process, and see what happens. Now I am not suggesting that you don't take consistent action. I'm simply saying that sometimes results come without effort, like with the free table. Written goals help you manage the coincidences in your life.

9. Written goals help you create the life of your dreams.

Why did you purchase this book? Why are you investing the time to learn these proven principles? Most people want to help create the life of their dreams.

How to Set Goals

I believe that the ten-step goal-setting process I am going to share with you is the most effective one in the world. When I designed this process, I wanted to combine the most effective goal-setting strategies with the easiest application. While I was creating this system, many of the processes I looked at were either too complicated or didn't give you enough information to be effective. The following system is designed with you in mind. Follow the ten simple steps in order to turn your dreams into reality.

The Ten-Step Goal-Setting Process

1. Think about what you want, and write it down.
2. Decide exactly what you want, and write it down.
3. Make sure your goal is measurable.
4. Identify the specific reasons you want this goal, and write them down.
5. Establish a definite date for accomplishment of your goal, and write it down.
6. List the action steps you need to take to accomplish your goal, and write them down.
7. Create an action plan from your list of action steps, and write it down.
8. Take action.

9. Do something every day.

10. View your goals as often as possible.

Let's break down each of these steps.

1. Think about what you want, and write it down.

What is your dream? Where do you want to travel in your lifetime? How much money do you want to have when you retire? What would be the ideal job? The goal-setting process starts with thinking about what you want and how you want your life to be. One simple way to begin this process is to ask yourself questions.

I have learned that your mind works like a search engine on the Internet. When you are on the Internet, you might go to a search engine such as Google. On Google you can search for websites just like you can search for companies in a phone book. When you make a search on Google, you type in the word, then Google will search for matching websites.

Your brain is like a search engine, too. When you ask it a question such as, "What would be the ideal job?" your brain will search through its files and produce an answer. One way to effectively think about what you want is to ask yourself questions about what you want. When you get the answers, write them down. There is no right way to think about what you want. The ideas will become a menu of choices from which you can create your goals. We call this menu the thought menu. You want as many choices as possible.

2. Decide exactly what you want, and write it down.

The second step in goal setting is to decide exactly what you want. Look at your thought menu. From this menu of ideas, take each idea to its completion. Be as specific as you can. For example, "I want to earn $100,000 over the next twelve months." Notice that my goal was not, "I want to make more money next year." That would not be specific enough. Say that I'm overweight and chronically tired. I look at my thought menu to come up with these goals:

I want to feel energized when I wake up in the morning.

My ideal body weight is 185 pounds.

I want to eat more fruits and vegetables.

I will avoid fast food, ice cream, and soda.

From the thought menu I want to take the idea to its completion. I decide the specific goal I want is to weigh 185 pounds. I now weigh 238. My goal is to lose fifty-three pounds.

3. Make sure your goal is measurable.

For a goal to be a goal, it must be written down. Once you have written it down, look at your goal to see if it is measurable. What I mean by measurable is that you will know when you have accomplished your goal. In our example, my goal is to weigh 185 pounds, or to lose fifty-three pounds. It is measurable, so it passes the test. If my goal were not measurable, then I would go back to Step 2 and rewrite the goal, making sure that it is measurable.

4. Identify the specific reasons you want this goal, and write them down.

The reason most people fail to achieve their goals is that they don't have a compelling enough reason to achieve them. Once you have begun the ten-step goal-setting process, you are ready to take action. Along the path toward achieving your goals, you will run into obstacles. That is where your "why" comes in. If your reason for achieving the goal is greater than the obstacles you face, then you will be much more likely to achieve the goal. Here is an example: You have been smoking a pack of cigarettes per day for eighteen years. For the past six years you have had the goal to stop smoking because you know smoking isn't good for you. You followed proper goal-setting techniques. You tried hypnosis, chewing nicotine gum, and quit-smoking seminars. Nothing seems to work. You go to the doctor. The doctor says you have lung cancer, and that if you quit smoking now, you will have ten years to live, but if you keep smoking, you will die in one year. Would you be able to quit smoking? I think most people would. Even though you had tried for the past six years and weren't able to succeed, I believe most people would be able to quit. Why? Because now they have a strong enough reason to accomplish the goal.

When you set a goal, look at why you want to achieve the goal. Is your why a big enough reason for you to overcome the obstacles to achieving your goal? If you don't have a strong enough reason, then imagine one. Spend some time really thinking about what it would mean to you to accomplish the goal. Also think about what the consequences will be if you don't accomplish the goal.

Write a paragraph about why you will successfully achieve your goal. Once you have completed the paragraph, read it over. After reading the paragraph, ask yourself the question, "Do I have a big enough why to overcome the obstacles I am going to encounter?"

Going back to my weight-loss example here is my why: I must lose fifty-three pounds because this is not the person I really am. I am sick and tired of people thinking of me as fat. I want to run a marathon before I die, and I will never be able to do it at this weight.

I then look at my **why** paragraph. I believe I have a strong enough why to overcome the obstacles I am going to face, so I continue with the process. If my why is not compelling enough, I must go back and rewrite it.

5. Establish a definite date for accomplishment of your goal, and write it down.

It is very important to decide when you want to accomplish your goal. Your mind has an unconscious timeline in it. For example, if your goal is to graduate from college by the end of 2017, your mind needs to start working on plans for how you will graduate by then. Knowing when you want to accomplish your goal will also have an effect on how you plan to achieve your goal. For example, if your goal is to earn $100,000 in the next twelve months, that is very different from having a goal of earning $100,000 any time in the future. Once you write down a date for your goal, your mind will start working toward achieving your goal. The only way to take advantage of your mind is to set a date and enter it into your subconscious by writing it down.

6. List the action steps you need to take to accomplish your goal, and write them down.

Ask yourself this question: What are all of the steps I need to take to accomplish my goal? This is a brainstorming exercise. We're looking to capture as many ideas as possible. We call this the action steps menu. Once again, we want as many choices as possible to create our plan. We are not looking for the steps to be in order at this point. Take out a clean sheet of paper and write anything and everything that comes to mind—things you will need to do in order to achieve your goal. Here is my action steps menu for our weight loss example:

- Go to the health food store to get good food.
- Exercise three times per week.
- Take a multi-vitamin every day.
- Meet with a nutrition expert to establish a diet.

- Meet with an exercise specialist to create a workout program.

- Create a tracking system to track my results.

- Buy an exercise book.

- Talk to my friend Bob (Bob lost thirty pounds) to find out how he lost weight.

Notice that the list is not in any particular order. This is a brainstorming session. I am looking to capture as many ideas as I can on paper. Once I've noted as many ideas as I can think of, I will then go to the next step.

7. Create an action plan from your list of action steps, and write it down.

Step 7 is where your thoughts mesh into a plan. Look at your action steps from Step 6. Now, put those ideas in sequential order: first do this, then that, and so on. In other words, simply prioritize the action steps you listed in Step 6. Do not let the word "plan" scare you. This is a simple exercise. Here's how this might look:

1. Talk to my friend Bob (Bob lost 30 pounds) and find out how he lost weight.

2. Buy an exercise book.

3. Make an appointment to meet with a nutrition expert to establish a diet.

4. Make an appointment to meet with an exercise specialist to create a workout plan.

5. Meet with the nutrition expert.

6. Go to the health food store to get good food.

7. Take a multi-vitamin every day.

8. Meet with the exercise specialist.

9. Create a tracking system to track my results.

10. Exercise three times per week.

When many people consider creating an action plan, they think of a lengthy process. The word "plan" scares them. As you can see from the above example, the plan took only a few minutes of thought. When you create a plan to achieve a goal, you need to ask yourself, "If I follow the plan, will I achieve the goal?" So in our example, if we execute the plan, would we lose fifty-three pounds in two years? The answer is yes.

8. Take action.

Every step in the ten-step goal-setting process is important. Each step depends upon the others. This step, however, could be the most important. I can't tell you how many educated derelicts I have met over the years—you know, the person who knows everything about everything, yet can't seem to get himself to take action on his own life. Goals and plans are great, but they alone don't produce results.

The only thing that produces results is action. How many times have you planned to do something . . . yet when it came to the action phase, you didn't act? You must get yourself to take consistent action on a daily basis—even if these actions are tiny baby steps. Remember: inch by inch, it's a cinch. When you take action on a consistent basis, even in small increments, you take advantage of the law of momentum, which states that once a body is in motion, it tends to stay in motion.

In our weight-loss example, one action I might take today would be to go to the health food store and pick out some healthy food. While small, it's still a positive step toward achieving my goal. Plus, it will help me create momentum. Another step I might take would be to jog for two minutes today. Now, two minutes might not seem like a lot, but to someone out of shape and overweight, it is. Most people never achieve their goals because they never take the first step. They never benefit from the law of momentum. Remember, the journey of a thousand miles begins with just one step. Inch by inch, it's a cinch.

9. Do something every day.

Work toward the achievement of your goals every day—even if it is a small step. Just as Rome wasn't built in a day, your major life goals aren't going to happen overnight in most cases. Practice patience.

In our weight-loss example, meeting with Bob to learn how he lost weight will help activate the law of momentum. By taking this small step today, I have put the law of momentum in my favor.

10. View your goals as often as possible.

Out of sight, out of mind. Human beings don't have the best memories. You have invested time to complete steps one through nine. Now that your goals are written down with a plan, you can quickly review five to ten goals in a matter of minutes. The more frequently you view your goals, the more you will burn them into your subconscious mind. Something magical happens when you do that. After some time of frequently reviewing your goals with their plans of action, your subconscious mind will start to believe you are going to achieve the goal. Once you have accomplished that, you can take advantage of the most powerful personal development idea ever discovered: **We become what we think about**.

Notice, with the exception of Step 8 (take action), every step requires that you think about what you want. Remember: We become what we think about. This is one of the secrets of this ten-step process. The process requires that you invest time thinking about what you want most in your life. Many people who do not achieve their goals invest their time thinking of all the reasons they can never succeed in their lives, or they invest their time thinking of ways to solve other people's problems, or they invest their thinking time in the fact that they have no money. Note there is nothing wrong with thinking about these things. However, if you choose to invest your time thinking in that way, just realize the consequences. Remember: We become what we think about.

Ideas Into Action

You have just learned the most powerful goal-setting process in the world. Now I would like to extend a challenge to you to take action—to implement these proven principles and create the life of your dreams. Good luck!

Key Points Review

- Your goals must be written down.

- There are many reasons why people don't set goals—don't fall into these traps.

- Follow my ten-step goal-setting plan to achieve your goals.

- Planning and goal setting alone are not enough—you must take action.

- Remember: We become what we think about.

Bonus Chapter #2

Time Management Success System

I've been fascinated with time management for many years. While I consider myself a time expert now, that wasn't always the case. In my early twenties, I was a cook at McDonald's earning $5.00 an hour. I would spend one hour working to make $5.00. That's what an hour was worth to me. A lot has changed since my time at McDonalds. One of the things that's changed the most is my understanding of time.

Here's a simple way to explain time management: Time management is about time *choices*. The better time choices you make, the more successful you'll become. I chose to spend a great deal of time writing and publishing this book. I believe this is a great time choice, because there's a future value to the time that I spent writing and publishing. Not only do I have the potential for financial gain from book sales, but I also have the knowledge and satisfaction that people will be reading and benefiting from this chapter for many, many years to come.

The Time Management Mindset

As with almost every other sales element discussed previously, you must develop the proper time management mindset from the beginning to make time management work for you. Many people believe that they're not good at time management. They believe that they're great at procrastinating. Instead, say the following affirmations each day to improve your time management inner game (you can say each every day, or say one over and over and then switch later on):

- Each day, I'm getting better and better at time management.
- I am a master of action.
- I am a time management master.
- I consistently plan my day before the day starts.

Years ago, during a time management discussion in a seminar, one of my students, Joey Azsterbaum, raised his hand and told me flat-out that he had terrible time management skills. I said, "Joey, if you say it like that, I believe you. So, do you want to improve your time management?"

He said yes, so I suggested that he use the following affirmations over and over each day:

> *I am a time management master.*
>
> *He is a time management master.*
>
> *Joey is a time management master.*

Why did I have Joey say this three different ways? Dr. Moine taught me that if you affirm it in the third person, as well as with your name in the first person, it impacts the subconscious mind in a different way.

A few months later, when another one of my clients met Joey, he was amazed at his efficiency and action, so he asked Joey how he was able to be so productive. Joey said, "Well, it's quite simple—I'm a time management master." He had literally reprogrammed his subconscious to believe that he is a master of time management. If you ever meet Joey, you can ask him about that, and he will tell you that he is a master of time management.

Time Management Truths

Once you have the proper time management mindset, you can delve into what I consider key time management truths:

- We all have the same amount of time.
- Time can have a future value. Take a bank, for example. Say a bank guarantees you a 2% return on your investment. If you put $100 into your account, one year from today, you'll have $102. Money can have a

future value. Well, so can time. In other words, you can invest time in activities today that you will benefit from later (and, in some cases, benefit from over and over again, for years to come).

- Some activities produce better results than others.

Let's look at these truths in a little more detail. As I began to learn more and more about time, I discovered the importance of understanding the value of an hour.

Annual income	Hours/ year	Income/ hour	Additional annual revenue from 1 extra hour of productivity per day (= 5 extra hours/week = 250 hours/year)	Additional revenue over 10 years from 1 extra hour of productivity per day
$50,000	2,000	$25	$6,250	$62,500
$100,000	2,000	$50	$12,500	$125,000
$1,000,000	2,000	$500	$125,000	$1,250,000

To calculate the worth to you of an hour financially, take the number of hours that you work a year and divide this number by how much money you earn. Generally speaking, if you work full-time, you work 2,000 hours per year (fifty weeks a year times forty hours a week). If you earn $100,000 a year and you work 2,000 hours per year, an hour is worth $50 to you. (Please calculate your hours, as some of you work more than forty hours, while some work less than forty hours.)

Understanding an hour's financial worth to you provides a great starting point for you to begin to make better time management choices. The person who cleans my home charges me $75 for each visit. It probably takes her and her crew three hours to complete the job. If I was to do the work myself, and it took me three hours, then I'd be earning $25 an hour. An hour to me is much more valuable than $25—hence, that's why I hire her and her team to do it. Here's a key time management principle that focuses directly on this idea of understanding your value of an hour:

Do what you do best and pay others to do the rest.

Pretty simple, huh? Yet you'll be amazed at how understanding the value of an hour will help you prioritize tasks and activities.

Time Management Systems

I strongly believe everyone should have a time management system. When I first began looking for a time management system, I focused on ones that already existed. Here's what I found (maybe you've found the same thing): pre-built time management systems tend to be complicated. They're hard to implement; they're not practical. And in most cases, they require a special day planner or special software. In looking at all the time management systems that I could find, I just couldn't find one that worked for me. So I created my own time management system.

I want to strongly encourage you to try my system. My system is practical, easy to implement, and will work for anyone at any age, regardless of what they do (even students can use this). If you like my time management system, I encourage you to share this system with others who can benefit as well.

And do you know the best part of my time management system? It's free. That's right—it doesn't require you to spend any money. I believe that if you apply my time management system, you will earn back a minimum of an extra hour of production every business day for the rest of your life. If the value of an hour for you is $25 an hour, an extra hour of production would be $25 times 250 hours per year, or an additional $6,250 over the next twelve months. That's pretty powerful. And the more you make, the more you'll benefit from this system.

Complete these steps to implement my time management system:

Step #1: Spend fourteen minutes a day planning your day on paper, in writing.

You can do this the night before, or in the morning before you begin your work. It doesn't matter when you do it, only that you plan. Why fourteen minutes? If you take twenty-four hours in a day and multiply that by sixty minutes in an hour, you'll get 1,440 minutes. One percent of 1,440 minutes is fourteen minutes, so one percent of your day is fourteen minutes, and it makes great sense to me to spend one percent of your day planning. Some people say, "Eric, I don't have fourteen minutes a day to plan." It's a paradox: I believe that every minute that you spend planning produces four minutes of results. Thus your fourteen minutes of planning produces fifty-six minutes of increased results. (If you're still having trouble believing that you have fourteen minutes a day to plan, review the earlier section on mindset.)

Step #2: During your fourteen minutes of planning, ask and answer key questions in writing.

Think about it; if you were going to plan today or tomorrow, you would do it by asking yourself a series of questions, such as these:

> What appointments do I have?
>
> Who do I need to follow up with?
>
> What is my goal for today?

Over time I created a series of questions I can ask myself to plan an optimal day. Here they are:

1. What level am I committed to playing at today?
2. How much time will I spend planning?
3. Where are my best opportunities right now?
4. How can I market to my database today to generate leads?
5. What are my goals today?
6. Look at my recipe box today.
7. How can I make $10,000 today?
8. What systems can I optimize today?
9. How can I create leverage today?
10. What can I spend 1 hour on that will make the biggest difference?
11. What must I accomplish today?
12. Who do I need to follow up with?
13. How can I produce the most revenue today?
14. How can my team produce the most revenue today?
15. Does my sales team have enough leads?
16. What will I do spiritually today?
17. What will I do for Jarris today?
18. What will I do for Brandon and Sarah today?

19. What will I do for my health today?
20. Apply the 80/20 rule to my plan: what are my two most valuable outcomes today?

I encourage you to use my list of questions as a template, or starting point, and then over time create your own customized list of questions to plan an optimum day. I have my questions stored on my computer under a file called "Time Management Questions for The Day."

Also, as much as possible, make this a no-distraction time. When I begin my fourteen minutes of planning, I don't check my cell phone, I don't send text messages, I don't read my email, I don't munch on a snack. I focus all of my energy on planning.

Step #3: After you've answered your questions, apply the 80/20 rule to your plan.

The 80/20 rule as it applies to selling simply states that, if you had a sales force of 100 people, the top twenty sales people, in theory, would produce results equal to the bottom eighty combined. The 80/20 rule also applies to ideas. And I believe it also applies to time management. Here's how. After you've made a list of what you want to accomplish for the day, review your list and then identify the top 20 percent of the items listed that, when completed, will provide you with the most value. For simplicity, I look at my planned list of activities and put an asterisk by the two activities that, when completed, will provide me with the most value. Then I focus my day on those two things.

This helps immensely those who dislike "not getting to everything." Now you can still list all of the activities you need to do, but you can feel good about only doing a few (the most important). I rarely get everything done on my daily list—which is why identifying the most valuable activities is so important.

To review, in order for you to implement my time system, you must spend fourteen minutes each day in planning, use my questions along with your own to plan your optimum day, and then prioritize the tasks and activities listed using the 80/20 rule. If you consistently do this system day in and day out every business day for the rest of your career, you will see a significant increase in your results. For the average person, I believe that consistently implementing this system will increase your financial results a minimum of $250,000 between now and the end of your career. (Some of you will get a far greater benefit.)

Leverage

Remember my client Joey Aszterbaum, who became a time management expert? Joey has also gotten very good at *leverage*. Leverage is one of the most important aspects of time management. Leverage is doing more with less. One of the most fascinating concepts that I've ever learned about leverage is what I call "infinite time," which can be summed up here:

Sometimes an hour is worth less than an hour in terms of results.

Sometimes an hour is equal to an hour in terms of results.

Sometimes an hour is greater than an hour in terms of results.

Most people think of an hour simply as sixty sequential minutes. When you look at time that way, time becomes fixed and limited. If you change the way you view time, however—if you change the way that you measure time—it can produce a whole new way of thinking about time. I call this infinite time. Instead of measuring time in terms of minutes per hour, you measure time in terms of *results per hour.*

Let me give you an example. If I watch television for an hour, I invested one hour and received zero results in terms of productivity. If I can make twenty phone calls in an hour, and I spend an hour making twenty phone calls, I invested one hour of time and I produced twenty phone calls, which is one hour of results. Now as I'm writing this book right now, the whole project will probably take me 250 hours, and the book will sell one hundred thousand copies, a million copies, ten million copies; time will tell how many copies it sells. I'm going to get a far greater return on my 250 hours of investment than simply 250 hours of result.

Here's another way to look at this. When I give a speech to a hundred people in the audience, how many hours of result have I produced? I've produced one hundred hours of results. I invested one hour and I got one hundred hours of results—each person (all one hundred) benefited from my one-hour speech). This is infinite time.

This concept gets better! There are ways of producing results where you invest no time. For example, you may end up meeting someone at some point and referring them to one of my mini websites, such as **www.7secretstosales-greatness.com**. Say the person went there, liked what she saw, and ended up purchasing one of my $49 CD sets. Great results, and how much time did I invest? Zero. When you produce a result and divide it into zero, you get infinity. That is a powerful concept, and I want you to know that you can do the exact same thing.

This idea can change your life. It sure changed mine. Here's how: I started my company from a spare bedroom in my condo with about $5,000 in the bank. I had no administrative support, a poor website, and a bad business plan. I had very little going for me at that point except an idea to change the way that the world sells. I was able to build a multi-million dollar global sales training organization from that spare bedroom in my condo using leverage and the concept of infinite time.

Let me give you a couple of examples of how to implement this idea.

Take email marketing. Let's say that it takes you fifteen minutes to write the email. You can send it to one person and get fifteen minutes of results, or you can send it to a hundred people and get 1,500 minutes of results. Or you could hire an assistant who works, say, twenty hours per week. You'd be getting twenty hours of result per week without investing any of your time. Nice, huh?

A written sales script also is a form of leverage. You must take the time at the beginning to get your sales script perfected, but once you've done that, you can benefit from it for the rest of your life.

Other Time Management Ideas

One of my best time management ideas is the file on my computer called "Best Ideas Right Now." I collect great ideas like some people collect baseball cards or stamps. When I hear a good idea, or I read or I see one, I immediately type it in to permanently record that great idea. I want to encourage you to create a file on your computer called "Best Ideas Right Now."

Here's another idea, a concept called "everything counts". This strategy will help you take more action because one of the reasons that people don't take action is they think "it won't matter." I live in a two-story home. I like to drink tea at night. Before I go to bed, I think to myself, "Should I take the teacup down and put it in the sink, or should I just leave it up here?" My initial thought is, it's only one teacup, it's not going to matter. But then I give myself the direct command—"Everything counts"—and I grab that teacup and I take it down to the kitchen sink.

I have told myself, "Everything counts" more than 500 times, and every time it's motivated me to take more action. Everything counts. Every time you read a page in this book, it counts. Every audio CD or MP3 you listen to counts. Every phone call counts.

The last time management idea I want to share with you is "focus on completion versus perfection." Many people don't take action because of a fear that what they produce won't be perfect. Several years ago, a gentleman named Andrew Duggan hired me to do telemarketing for his company. At the time, he had the idea to take content providers (people like myself, with sales training content), and use their content to create online training modules. He hired me to contact content providers (well-known instructors) and secure them as clients. They would give their content, and in return Andrew would do a revenue share with them.

I said, "Andrew, here's what going to happen. I'm going to get on the phone to, say, Zig Ziglar [who passed away recently while I was writing this], and I'm probably going to get Zig's assistant. She'll ask me to send some information. Do you have a marketing piece that we can send out to these content providers?" Andrew said no, so I suggested that he hire a copywriter.

He said, "Could you do it?"

"I could, but I'm not a copywriter," I replied. "But you really need to have a professional copywriter do it."

"But *can* you do it?" he pressed.

"Yeah, I could do it. It won't probably be that good, but I could do it."

"Great," said Andrew, "you go ahead and do it."

So I created a marketing piece. Sure enough, all the content providers wanted me to fax (this was in the pre-email era) the information. One day Andrew got on the phone with Robert Allen, author of *Nothing Down*, who asked for the information. Andrew faxed it to Robert.

The next day, Robert called up Andrew and said, "I saw the document and I'm interested in talking with you further about your project. But let me ask you a question: Who wrote the fax piece?"

"Eric Lofholm wrote it," Andrew replied. "Why?"

"That fax piece is horrible," said Robert bluntly. "Tell guy who wrote it to call me, so I can tell him how to fix it."

I called Robert Allen and he gave me two free, one-hour coaching sessions to help fix the fax piece. That's an example of Focus on Completion versus Perfection. It's a simple idea and it's a profound idea.

Ideas Into Action

Throughout this book I've given plenty of techniques and ideas to make more sales. As you get busier and your business grows, time management will come to play an even greater role in your ongoing success. Take the time (!) now to put a proper time management system into place, and then follow it every day. The results will pay you back many, many times over.

Key Points Review

- Develop the right time management mindset.

- Realize that time has a future value.

- Calculate the worth of an hour for you.

- Implement and use a time management system (I recommend my own!).

- Believe that "everything counts" in your personal and work life.

Bonus Chapter #3

Lofholmisms

The "Lofholmisms" in this chapter are some key teachings, concepts, and sayings I repeat frequently for reinforcement. I also call these "distinctions." These are a few phrases and concepts you'll probably hear me say and refer to over and over. Keep an ear open for them when you listen to me, and keep an eye out for these as you read this book, and this will help you absorb my teaching on a deeper level.

- Stay in the conversation
- Ask, ask, ask
- Z strategy
- Phase 1 2 3 4
- Interview with the Experts
- Rapport reduces resistance
- Elegantly dance with the prospect
- Intuitive upsell
- GSA
- 80/20
- Do what you know
- Optimization
- Automation

- Digital Eric
- Precession
- Repetition
- Business sky hook
- Bread and butter
- 7+
- Level 10

Top 150 Secrets
of Success

If you've read other sales books and how-to books like Wiley's *For Dummies* series, you've probably seen a lot of them give you lists of top 10 tips. Some give you 20. A few even give you 100 or more. I believe in overdelivery, so in this bonus chapter I'm going to give you not 10, not 20, not even 100, but 150 of my top secrets to achieving success in sales and other areas of life. I call them "golden nuggets" because they're more valuable than gold. Some of the tips in this chapter are worth hundreds of thousands or even millions of dollars or more to the right person. You will find that this chapter alone is worth many times the price you paid for this book. Come back to it often to refresh your memory and inspire your imagination.

Top 10 Sales Success Secrets
1. Stay in the conversation
2. Cultivate a mindset for sales success
3. Use multiple sales systems
4. Focus on strategic lead targets
5. Use a database
6. Rehearse your sales scripts

7. Ask questions throughout your presentation

8. Sell the benefit of the benefit

9. Set specific sales goals

10. Schedule actions for successful execution

1. Stay in the conversation

Stay in the conversation is the #1 distinction I teach. It means to keep learning from me (or any other mentor you study under). It also means to keep applying what you learn by taking action. It means to keep studying this book. It means to take advantage of other training opportunities I offer, like my training videos, teleseminars, webinars, and seminars.

Why is this the #1 distinction I teach? Because the longer you stay in the conversation, the more you will learn, and the more value you will get out of what you learn. After 100 hours of training with me you will know the key distinctions I teach. This will give us a foundation for taking our conversation to a new level of understanding and practical application. You will look back at things we discussed at the beginning of your training and you will see it in a new light. For instance, you will be ready to apply the general model of Sales Mountain to specific industries like public speaking, coaching, and network marketing, multiplying your income potential enormously.

2. Cultivate a mindset for sales success

I started off Chapter 1 by talking about sales mindset. I started there because sales mindset is important! Your mindset sets the stage for your results, so it's important not to skip over the mindset exercises I taught you in Chapter 1.

Remember the law of belief: what you tell yourself over and over eventually comes true. Tell yourself over and over that selling equals service; selling comes from honesty, integrity, and compassion; selling is about leading and about moving people to action. Use these affirmations to help you embrace selling. Create a list of positive affirmations for all other parts of your life that can impact your sales, including your health, your relationships, and your spirituality.

Mindset also includes committing to playing at a 7+ every day. Play at a 10 as often as you can, but commit to playing at least at a 7 every day. Make this commitment to push yourself to levels of success you didn't believe were possible.

3. Use multiple sales systems

My marketing mentor Jay Abraham, one of the top five marketing consultants in the corporate world according to *Forbes*, taught me that one of the keys to business success is using multiple sales systems. You should strive to have multiple sales systems for each phase of selling, including lead generation, appointment booking, and sales presentations. For each of these areas, you can deploy multiple sales systems in multiple media. For instance, your lead generation systems might include traditional systems like referrals, direct mail, and advertising as well as contemporary systems like email marketing, social media, and video marketing. The more sales systems you have in place, the more leads you will generate, the more appointments you will book, and the more sales presentations you will deliver and close.

4. Focus on strategic lead targets

If you want to catch fish, you have to cast your line where the fish are. If you want to make more sales, you should focus your lead generation efforts where your target market is. An example of this is the Person of Influence (POI) strategy I discussed back in Chapter 4. When you influence a POI to promote you to their network, you can generate many leads from influencing that one POI in a fraction of the time it would take you to generate that many leads on your own, potentially reaching hundreds, thousands, or even millions of people through one POI. This is an example of focusing on a strategic lead target. Go back and review Chapter 4 for other ideas about ways to make your lead generation efforts more strategic.

5. Use a database

For many years I resisted using an email database. I thought it was too much work. Finally a smart friend of mine who was making a lot of money from email marketing convinced me, "Eric you need to start using a database." Today I am so grateful for that advice, because my database is one of my most reliable, most profitable marketing tools.

Make sure that any time you get a lead, whether it's through email, a business card, a referral, or any other source, you enter it into your database. My database includes every single contact I've ever entered, along with information such as their contact information, what they've bought from me, and where they are in the sales cycle. My database helps keep me and my team in touch with my customer base and lets me and my sales reps prepare more effectively for presentations.

6. Rehearse your sales scripts

In Chapter 13 I told you that sales scripting is the most profitable idea I have ever learned out of all the thousands of sales ideas I've collected over the last twenty years. I always use prepared scripts during every one of my main sales presentations. Unfortunately, the best sales script in the world won't help you if you don't rehearse it! Make sure you take the time to rehearse your sales scripts. Practice your main scripts multiple times before each presentation. Think of how many times a baseball batter practices before each plate appearance. There are hundreds and thousands of swings behind each home run. Get your script "batting practice" in.

7. Ask questions throughout your presentation

In Chapter 7, I told you that one of the most effective ways you could improve your sales results was to prepare a list of powerful probing questions prior to your presentation to help you identify customer needs. You can enhance the power of questions by building questions into other parts of your presentation as well. In addition to identifying customer needs, you can use questions to build rapport, by asking questions as simple as, "How are you doing today?" You can ask questions to help you qualify your prospect, learn about their buying habits, or determine their budget. You can ask questions to help you anticipate which benefits they're interested in or which objections they're harboring. You can ask questions to respond to objections, as discussed in the chapter on objection handling. You can ask questions to generate referrals. You can even ask yourself questions! Asking yourself questions can help you with areas such as mindset, goal setting, and time management.

8. Sell the benefit of the benefit

In Chapter 8, I mentioned that the real reason why people buy is often not the obvious benefit, but the underlying benefit that I call the "benefit of the benefit." I gave the example of someone who buys my sales training program. Are they buying it because they want to learn sales? Maybe on the surface, but beneath that they want to learn sales because they want some other benefit that comes from making more sales.

So I might say to them, "Imagine you are now a sales champion. How will your life be different? What kind of car will you be driving?" They usually say something like, "Oh, when I am a sales champion, I'll be driving this kind of car." This connects them with the fact that the benefit of making more sales gives them the more compelling benefit of driving the car they've always wanted: the benefit of the benefit.

Get in the habit of thinking in terms of the benefit of the benefit. You will find that this exponentially increases the appeal of the benefits section of your sales presentation. And soon you'll be making enough sales to drive the car *you* want.

9. Set specific sales goals

When you're setting sales goals, you'll get better results if you aim for specific target numbers. Saying "I plan to make more sales" is less specific than "I plan to make ten cold calls a day this week" or "I plan to book twenty appointments this month" or "I plan to make thirty sales a month this year." The more specific you set your goals, the better you can plan your strategy and take appropriate action. You may fall short of your goals, or you may exceed them, but either way, having a specific goal gives you a better chance to make corrective adjustments.

10. Schedule actions for successful execution

What doesn't get scheduled doesn't get done, I've found. A key to turning plans into results is committing blocks of time to taking action. Declaring your intention by setting a schedule is the first step towards taking action. There's a power in putting your plans to paper and declaring your intent to act.

Top 10 Sales Mistakes to Avoid

1. Don't neglect your inner game
2. Don't rely on just one lead generation system
3. Don't neglect your database
4. Don't try to sell when you're trying to generate a lead
5. Don't try to sell when you're trying to book an appointment

6. Don't wing it

7. Don't forget to maintain rapport

8. Don't sell features

9. Don't try to close prematurely

10. Don't let perfectionism become procrastination

1. Don't neglect your inner game

It's easy to get so focused on the sales process and your outer game that you forget to practice your inner game. This is a mistake, because it fails to build the confident mindset you need to practice your outer game successfully. If you feel nervous about selling because you haven't internalized the idea that selling is a service, it's going to hurt your ability to establish rapport. If you're afraid to ask for a sale, it's going to diminish your ability to close. Address these problems by practicing your inner game to sharpen your outer game.

2. Don't rely on just one lead generation system

Earlier I mentioned Jay Abraham's advice to use multiple sales systems, including multiple lead generation systems. The opposite of this is to rely exclusively on one lead generation system to get new customers, such as spontaneous word-of-mouth referrals, directory listings, or advertising.

This can get your business into trouble. For one thing, if your main source of leads dries up, where will you get new leads? And without new leads, what will happen to your sales and revenue?

Besides this, relying exclusively on one lead generation system is limiting your business. It keeps you from testing other tools that might generate more leads if you tried them. It also keeps you from testing which lead generation tool is the most effective one to use for your market. You may find that another lead generation tool generates ten or a hundred times more leads than the one you're using, but you'll never know until you test it.

3. Don't neglect your database

I've emphasized how important it is to maintain a database. But once you get a database, don't neglect to use it! For instance, you'd be surprised how many Internet marketers create squeeze pages and build a mailing list, only to never sell their list anything. Another common mistake is only selling to your list one time and then never offering them anything new. And don't forget you can also use your list to ask for referrals!

4. Don't try to sell when you're trying to generate a lead

The purpose of lead generation is to generate a lead: to get a new name added to your database contact list. The purpose of lead generation is not to close a sale.

After reading this book you already know this, but the vast majority of sales representatives stumble over this distinction. They try to close the deal immediately during their first contact with the contact, skipping steps like appointment booking and establishing customer needs in their haste to close the sale. How many times have you gotten sales calls from someone trying to sell you something you never expressed an interest in? How often does that work? Not too often, right?

So don't make that mistake. When you're trying to generate a lead, focus on generating a lead. Focus on collecting your prospect's contact information. Save the sales presentation for the right time.

5. Don't try to sell when you're trying to book an appointment

This next tip is like the last one. The purpose of appointment booking is to book an appointment: to commit your prospect to scheduling a sales presentation. The purpose of appointment booking is not to deliver the sales presentation you're trying to book. Don't put the cart before the horse here, either.

6. Don't wing it

Tom Hopkins, the greatest real estate salesman who ever lived, wrote in his book *How to Master the Art of Selling*, "Salespeople like to wing it. That is to say, average salespeople like to wing it. Champions like to make money. So they don't wing it—they prepare. Intensively."

7. Don't forget to maintain rapport

I put building trust and rapport at the beginning of the steps in the sales mountain sales presentation section. However, building rapport is one thing, keeping it is another. Just because you've built rapport doesn't automatically guarantee you'll hold it throughout your presentation. Failing to ask questions, failing to convey benefits, failing to pace your close, failing to answer objections, failing to follow up can all disrupt the rapport you've worked so hard to build. Make sure you keep reinforcing rapport throughout your presentation.

This also applies if you have to follow up your initial presentation with a subsequent contact with the prospect. When you last talked to them they may have been ready for the close, but that doesn't necessarily mean that they're going to be ready to close the next time they pick up the phone with you. You don't know what happened that day before you called them. For all you know they're having a lousy day. Don't just jump back into your sales presentation with a close. Check for rapport first, and lead your prospect back up Sales Mountain before going for the close again. You probably won't need to deliver your full presentation all over again, but you may need to jog their memory by hitting the highlights to get them back in the right mood.

8. Don't sell features

Benefits sell; features don't; but despite this, most sales representatives try to sell features. This is one reason most sales representatives struggle. They get so caught up talking about their product or service that they shift the focus away from how their product or service can benefit their prospect. Avoid this problem by keeping the focus on customer needs and selling benefits to meet those needs, not features.

9. Don't try to close prematurely

Famed actor Orson Welles once did a commercial for a wine company that promised, "We will sell no wine before its time." It takes a fine wine time to age to just the right maturity with the right aroma and taste. Selling the wine prematurely diminishes its quality and appeal. The same is true of a premature close. Don't rush to close before you've performed the prior steps of establishing trust and rapport, identifying customer needs, and presenting benefits. When you do get to the close, take it step-by-step as well, putting the pieces together one at a time before you ask for the sale. Close no sale before its time.

10. Don't let perfectionism become procrastination

I teach my students to focus on completion, not perfection. There is a time and a place for perfection, but when it comes to motivating action, completion is more important than perfection. You can always improve something once you do something, but it's very hard to improve nothing. Waiting to start until you're perfect is a recipe for procrastination. To get into action, focus on completion, not perfection.

Top 10 Sales Mindsets

I've stressed how important mindset is to sales success. Your mindset is influenced by what you tell yourself over and over, which influences your beliefs. Here are ten things you can tell yourself over and over through affirmations to build a successful sales mindset.

1. Selling is something everyone does in daily life
2. Selling is a learned skill
3. Selling equals service
4. Selling provides value
5. People want to buy from you
6. Selling is a system
7. Selling is easy
8. Selling is easiest when you rehearse
9. Selling improves with practice
10. You are a sales master

1. Selling is something everyone does in daily life

Have you ever influenced someone else to do something? Have you ever told your kids to do something? Have you ever gotten your husband, wife, boyfriend, or girlfriend to do something for you? Have you ever persuaded a coworker to do you a favor? Then you've sold something. Selling is something everyone does in their daily life. When you realize this, sales can be less scary. If the Girl Scouts can do it, you can do it!

2. Selling is a learned skill

Selling is something just about anyone can learn. The idea that you have to be born with a special charisma to be successful at sales is a myth. Some of the

.nost successful sales representatives are perfectly ordinary people who simply take the time to listen to their customers, find out what they need, and help them find what they need. The cashier at McDonald's or the floor associate at Walmart is a salesperson. You don't have to be a born used car salesman to be successful at sales.

3. Selling equals service

Selling is performing the service of providing customers with something that benefits them. Selling isn't about arm-twisting, nagging, or being pushy. Selling equals service.

4. Selling provides value

Selling is about providing a value that meets the needs of your prospect. It isn't manipulating someone to buy something they don't need. It isn't about taking money in exchange for nothing. It's about providing value.

5. People want to buy from you

People buy things because they need them. If they don't buy them from you, they're going to have to find someone else to sell them what they need. This is extra work. Why wouldn't they want to save themselves the trouble and just buy it from you? People want to buy from you.

6. Selling is a system

Selling as a system means that selling is a step-by-step process that gets repeatable, consistent results. It isn't magic. It isn't rocket science. If you follow the same steps, you will get the same results, time after time. Selling is a system.

7. Selling is easy

Because selling is a system, because selling is something everyone does in daily life, because selling is a learned skill, selling can be easy. It doesn't have to be as hard as some people make it out to be. It can be as simple as asking, "Would you like to buy some Girl Scout Cookies?" "Would you like something to drink with that?" "Paper or plastic?"

8. Selling is easiest when you rehearse

Selling is easy, and it's easiest when you rehearse. If you were going to be in a play, you'd rehearse your lines, right? If you were going to play in a big baseball game, you'd practice batting before the game, wouldn't you? Rehearse your sales script in the same way and you'll find that selling can be as easy as laying down a bunt.

9. Selling improves with practice

Like most skills, selling improves with practice. Don't be dismayed if you don't close every sale when you're a beginner. Even sales masters don't usually close every sale. I don't! But my sales skills have gradually improved with practice. So will yours.

10. You are a sales master

Henry Ford once said, "Whether you think you can, or you think you can't, either way, you're right." If you tell yourself you're a sales master, you will eventually become a sales master.

Top 10 Lead Generation Ideas

1. The purpose of lead generation is to generate leads
2. Use a database to manage your leads
3. Leverage one-to-many lead generation opportunities
4. Use your database to generate referrals
5. Use joint venture partners to generate leads
6. Build relationships with persons of influence
7. Use public speaking opportunities to generate leads
8. Use social media to generate leads
9. Use technology to automate lead generation
10. Use multiple lead generation systems

1. The purpose of lead generation is to generate leads

I've said this before, but I'm going to repeat it because it's important: the purpose of lead generation is to generate leads. It's to add contacts to your database of prospects. It's not to book appointments. It's not to close sales. Realizing this will make your lead generation efforts much easier and less stressful.

2. Use a database to manage your leads

The best way to manage your leads is to enter them into a database. Use a spreadsheet program like Excel or customer relationship management (CRM) software that builds on spreadsheets, like Constant Contact. Enter each lead's contact information as well as other important information like what industry they're in, what they're interested in, what they've bought from you, and where they are in the sales cycle.

3. Leverage one-to-many lead generation opportunities

The most efficient way to generate leads is to seek opportunities that let you generate many leads at once instead of just one at a time. Examples are public speaking, webinars, and online content syndication. These types of lead generation methods enable you to get in front of many prospects at one time.

4. Use your database to generate referrals

One efficient way to generate leads is to use your database to generate referrals. Ask your database contacts to refer you to others in your target market. Chances are they know others like them who could also use your products or services.

5. Use joint venture partners to generate leads

Another highly-leveraged lead generation source is joint venture partners. Your JV partners are already in contact with customers in your target market, and may already have lead databases like the one you're trying to build. Instead of starting from scratch, influence your JV partners to promote you to their database. Using this method I'm able to extend the reach of my email marketing campaigns from my own list of tens of thousands of members to JV partner networks reaching as many as five million subscribers.

6. Build relationships with persons of influence

Working with JV partners who have their own mailing lists is an example of building relationships with persons of influence. Cultivate relationships with POIs who can help you generate leads by promoting you to their databases or assisting you in other ways, like helping you network with list owners or endorsing you in a way that adds credibility to your product or service in the eyes of your target audience.

7. Use public speaking opportunities to generate leads

A great way to generate multiple leads at one time is using public speaking opportunities. These include speeches, interviews, seminars, webinars, and podcasts.

8. Use social media to generate leads

Social media tools like Facebook, Twitter, and LinkedIn let you generate leads with demographic characteristics fitting your target market. For certain markets, social media marketing is one of the best ways to generate leads fast.

9. Use technology to automate lead generation

You don't have to do all your lead generation by hand. You can use technology to help you automate your lead generation system. Using a database for customer relationship management is one example. Another example is what I call "Digital Eric." I create videos of myself doing sales presentations that I can distribute by posting them online, emailing them to my mailing list, or having my affiliates and JV partners point others to them. This lets me sell digitally even when I'm physically doing something else.

10. Use multiple lead generation systems

The more lead generation systems you have in place, the more leads you will generate. Use multiple lead generation systems to multiply your leads. This will also keep your sales coming in even if one lead generation source dries up unexpectedly.

Top 10 Public Speaking Tips

I was fortunate to study public speaking under one of the great masters of our generation, Tony Robbins, who in turn had learned from the great Jim Rohn. One of the more advanced levels of my sales system includes a course that applies my sales strategies to public speaking. I normally charge several thousand dollars for the full course, which contains much more material than I can include here, but as a bonus for reading this book through to this point, here are ten of my top public speaking tips that you can put into practice immediately in your speaking opportunities.

1. Use public speaking for lead generation
2. Generate leads for your public speaking events
3. Book attendance for your public speaking events
4. Script your speeches
5. Rehearse your scripts
6. Use technology to extend your public speaking audience
7. Use the boss talk strategy to coordinate your public speaking events with your hosts
8. Use public speaking to book appointments
9. Use public speaking to sell
10. Record your public speaking events for reuse

1. Use public speaking for lead generation

Public speaking has always been one of my best lead generation strategies. I give several group talks a week, including both live events and remotely-attended events like teleseminars and webinars. By offering free information that people want, you create an incentive for them to give you their contact information. You can make the incentive even stronger by offering them a reward for providing their contact information, such as a recording of your talk or a PDF file containing a slideshow for your talk.

2. Generate leads for your public speaking events

To get people to attend your public speaking events, you also need to generate leads in order to send out invitations. You can achieve this by using any of the lead generation strategies discussed in this book, including online opt-in forms, social media invitations, and email marketing to your own mailing list and JV partners' lists.

3. Book attendance for your public speaking events

Just like when you're setting appointments for sales presentations, there is an appointment-setting process for booking public speaking events. The best practice is to get your invitees on a mailing list so you can send out instructions and reminders on how to attend. This also lets you follow up with additional invitations and sales opportunities.

4. Script your speeches

Surveys show that public speaking is near the top of most people's list of fears, along with death and taxes. Why are people so afraid of public speaking? One of the biggest reasons people get nervous is they don't know what they're going to say. Avoid this problem by scripting your speeches just like you script your sales presentations. If you watch the best public speakers, they deliver their main speeches the same way every time. Imitate their example to imitate their success.

5. Rehearse your scripts

There's a difference between having a great script and a great delivery. If I tried to read a scene from *Hamlet*, my delivery wouldn't sound as polished as a Shakespearian actor like Sir Ian McKellen would, because I haven't practiced the lines. Great delivery comes from great rehearsal. Practice your main scripts multiple times before each presentation and you will find the quality of your delivery improving dramatically.

6. Use technology to extend your public speaking audience

I recently took my public speaking technology to a new level by adopting a strategy I call "Digital Eric." Using prerecorded videos, with distribution help from my affiliates and joint venture partners, I'm able to deliver virtual sales presentations 24 hours a day. This enables me to reach many times the number of people I could reach through live presentations alone.

This is just one example of how technology can enable you to reach a wider audience than you could through live face-to-face presentations. Learn to use technological tools like video marketing, telemarketing, email marketing, social media, and mobile phones. Put the power of automation to work to leverage your sales results.

7. Use the boss talk strategy to coordinate your public speaking events with your hosts

When I'm organizing public speaking events where I'm not the host or presenter, I use a preparation technique called the "boss talk" that I learned from Tony Robbins. (It's called the "boss talk" because you're talking to the "boss" of the event.) Before giving the actual presentation, I have a talk with the event coordinator to cover some details crucial to running an effective speaking engagement. I confirm the event, find out details like how many people will be attending and what content they'd like, see if it's okay for me to end the meeting, and make sure the host doesn't have a problem with me making a sales offer at the end of the presentation. This prevents the type of awkward situation that can arise if I make an unexpected sales offer at the end of the presentation and everyone looks at the coordinator like, "Is the company paying for this?" Use the boss talk to make sure everything goes smoothly during presentations when you're not the host.

8. Use public speaking to book appointments

Besides using public speaking for lead generation, you can also use public speaking to book appointments. For instance, you can offer a free sales consultation to people who attend your speech, or perhaps to the first five people who respond if you need to limit it. You can extend this type of offer either at the end of your speech itself or as a follow-up offer to a lead generation offer. For instance, you could collect contact information by offering a free recording of your speech to people who email you, and then offer a free or discounted consultation to people who respond to this offer.

9. Use public speaking to sell

You can also use public speaking to sell. There are several ways to sell during your presentations. I often offer my sales training program at the end of my speeches, which is called "front-of-the-room selling." You can also sell from the "back of the room" by having a table where you offer books, videos, or other items your audience wants. Of course the table doesn't literally have to be at the back of the room, and if you're in a digital environment it doesn't even have to be a literal table! You can give people a link to a sales page, for example.

10. Record your public speaking events for reuse

Whenever possible, be sure to record your public speaking engagements so you can reuse them. Recordings make great lead-generation giveaway offers. They can also be sold as audio or video products, or transcribed into written products.

Sometimes if someone else is hosting your event, you may need to get permission to record your speech. For instance, if you're going on a talk radio show, make sure to bring this up with the host during your boss talk and ask them whether you will have the rights to distribute a recording. Often they will provide you with a recording if you ask.

Top 10 Phone Tips

I started my sales career making phone calls, and I've been doing it for the last twenty years. I've used the phone to generate millions of dollars worth of revenue. Here are ten of my top phone tips. (And by the way, the phone tips presented here can also be adapted to other communication technology that uses audio like online VoIP calls and videoconferencing tools such as Skype.)

1. Use the phone to generate leads
2. Use the phone to book appointments
3. Use the phone to sell
4. Script your phone calls
5. Practice your phone manner
6. Use teleseminars to practice your phone skills
7. Make sure you call the right person
8. Learn to deal with phone gatekeepers
9. Support phone calls with other media
10. Follow up on phone calls

1. Use the phone to generate leads

Telemarketing is so popular because the phone is one of the best lead generation tools out there. Phone directories provide you with a ready-made database you can use to start collecting not only phone numbers but also other related information like addresses, email addresses, and website information. You can use the phone to call consumers and businesses in your target market. You can also use the phone to generate leads by asking for referrals. Finally, you can use the phone to contact joint venture partners who can generate leads for you.

2. Use the phone to book appointments

The phone is a primary tool for booking appointments. Use the phone to offer appointments, confirm appointments, run appointments, and follow up on appointments.

3. Use the phone to sell

I have students who earn tens of thousands of dollars a month just by making phone calls from my office or their home. You can do the same thing if you master applying the Sales Mountain strategy to the phone. Learn to use the phone to build trust and rapport, ask probing questions, present benefits, deliver closes, handle objections, and follow up.

4. Script your phone calls

As with any sales presentation, you should always script your phone calls. This includes scripting calls that are designed for lead generation or appointment booking. Scripting your phone calls will help you avoid the cold-calling anxiety that terrorizes so many sales representatives. When you're prepared for your call, your anxiety level will drop dramatically. The more you practice, the more comfortable you'll get.

5. Practice your phone manner

As with public speaking, you should practice your delivery when using the phone. There are several ways to do this. One is to say your scripts out loud and pretend you're on the phone. Another is to practice with someone you know and trust. A third way is live calls. For best results, record your practice calls so you can evaluate your skills and see where you need to improve.

6. Use teleseminars to practice your phone skills

A great way to practice your phone skills is to participate in teleseminars, either as a participant or as a presenter. For instance, during my weekly training calls, I open the call by inviting people to say hello, which not only builds trust and rapport, but gives my students an opportunity to practice getting over phone anxiety. I also offer a question and answer session at the end of the call. Joining in calls like this where you can participate is a great way to hone your basic phone skills. As your confidence grows you can practice hosting your own calls. You don't even actually have to have anyone on the call to practice! Just talking to a live line is great practice.

7. Make sure you call the right person

When you're making calls to book appointments or deliver sales presentations, always make sure you're talking to the right person. For instance, if you want to schedule an appointment with an executive, you might need to make sure you talk to the right department and the right assistant to set up the appointment. Or if you're trying to sell something over the phone, make sure you're talking to a person with the authority to buy what you're selling. Otherwise you could end up successfully closing the sale only to have them tell you they need to talk to their spouse or boss.

8. Learn to deal with phone gatekeepers

Because you will often need to go through another person like a secretary to get on the phone with the right decision-maker, you should learn how to deal with phone "gatekeepers." The same persuasion skills that apply to closing a sale also apply to convincing a secretary to put you in touch with their boss. Make sure to build trust and rapport and follow the other steps in Sales Mountain to get them motivated to help you. Sometimes this can be as simple as being friendly and offering them the benefit of your appreciation for their help. Assistants work hard, and appreciate people who acknowledge their efforts. (I know how they feel: I used to be Dante Perano's assistant!)

9. Support phone calls with other media

You can often use the phone more effectively by leaning on other media for support. For instance, you might send an email on ahead of a phone call, or you might follow up a phone call with an email. I usually have my assistant send out an email to confirm a phone appointment. You can also use the phone in conjunction with other media like video links, social media, or regular mail.

10. Follow up on phone calls

One of the biggest keys to using the phone successfully is following up. You've probably heard that it can take as many as six or twelve or more phone calls to close a sale. Follow-up phone calls can also help you confirm details of an appointment, communicate important information between appointments, and follow up to get referrals.

Top 10 Email Tips

My email database has tens of thousands of names and is growing every day. My affiliates and joint venture partners have over five million subscribers. I can generate tens of thousands of dollars a day with the right email to my list. I know some people who generate millions of dollars a year primarily through email marketing. Here are ten ways you can use email to help you make more money.

1. Use email marketing to market to your database
2. Use email to generate leads
3. Use email to book appointments and send appointment reminders
4. Use email to sell
5. Address your emails personally
6. Use attention-grabbing subject lines
7. Get to the point
8. Close with a call to action
9. Include response instructions
10. Avoid spam

1. Use email marketing to market to your database

Sending emails to your own "in-house" customer database is one of the most efficient sales strategies you can implement. Your in-house mailing list already knows who you are, knows they can trust you, and knows the benefits of what you sell, so they're already more than halfway up Sales Mountain. Anti-spam regulations require you to get permission before mass emailing people, so you should gear your lead generation strategy towards collecting email addresses and getting prospects on your mailing list from Day One.

2. Use email to generate leads

Email can be a powerful lead generation tool. There are several ways you can use email to generate leads. One is to use opt-in incentives to get people to sign up for your mailing list. Another is to ask your list members to forward emails to others who might be interested in your products or events. A third is to get your affiliates and joint venture partners to invite others to visit your website, online events, or live events.

3. Use email to book appointments and send appointment reminders

Email can be an efficient way to book appointments and send out appointment reminders. You can automate this process by using tools that combine email with calendar programs like Outlook. If you use email for appointment booking, make sure the person you're trying to communicate with actually reads their email. Some people don't, in which case you need to find out a better way to contact them. Because of this, it's a best practice to request a reply when sending out an appointment-booking email.

4. Use email to sell

When you apply Sales Mountain, you can easily close sales right over the phone. The reason most sales representatives have a hard time closing on the phone is because they skip the Sales Mountain sequence, jumping right into the close without going through the previous steps. If you apply the same step-by-step system to phone calls that I teach for live presentations, you can deliver a well-scripted close over the phone as the natural conclusion to a well-delivered presentation.

5. Address your emails personally

Your emails will get a much better open rate if you address them personally. This makes you sound less like junk mail. Most people respond best to their first name. However in some business contexts or other social contexts, a title might be appropriate.

By the same token, you should usually use your own name when sending out emails. People respond better to a person with a name instead of a title like "admin" or a nickname they don't recognize.

6. Use attention-grabbing subject lines

After names, your subject line is the part of your email that first grabs your reader's attention and influences their decision whether to read your email or delete it. Increase your email's odds of being read by using a subject line that grabs your reader's attention. The same principles that apply when presenting benefits apply here. A good subject line typically asks an interesting question, addresses a need your reader has, or offers a benefit they want.

7. Get to the point

Long emails are hard to read and take up valuable time. You'll get a better response if you keep your emails short. If you need to include detailed information, it's best to include it as an attachment or a link. You can also use techniques like headers and bolding to break up long text.

8. Close with a call to action

Just as a sales presentation builds towards a close, an email should build towards what copywriters call the "call to action." The call to action is the action you want your reader to take after reading your email. A call to action might be emailing you back, calling you, or clicking on a link to go to an order form. Make sure your call to action is clear, and make sure the paragraphs preceding it set the stage for it.

9. Include response instructions

If your call to action requires your reader to contact you or take some other action like filling out an order form, make sure you include any instructions they'll need. For the best response, make your instructions as easy to follow as possible.

10. Avoid spam

When using email marketing techniques, it's important to follow anti-spam regulations to keep you from losing your mailing list service, getting fined, or getting in legal trouble. Always get permission from people through an opt-in form before adding them to your mailing list. Never share others' contact information without their permission. Your email service provider's website should have more detailed guidelines for avoiding spam.

Top 10 Social Media Tips

Over the past two years, I've been using social media more and more to grow my business. Facebook is one of the most valuable tools I use, helping me with lead generation, appointment booking, sales, and even running seminars and training my sales representatives. I'm also finding YouTube a great tool for connecting with prospects and customers through video. Here are some tips you can apply to generate more leads and make more sales using these social media tools as well as Twitter, LinkedIn, Pinterest, and others.

1. Use social media for lead generation
2. Use social media to book appointments
3. Use social media to set the stage for sales
4. Brand your social media pages
5. Customize your social media pages
6. Post on a regular schedule
7. Give others reasons to like and follow you
8. Give others reasons to click on your links
9. Use automated social media tools
10. Use analytics to track your results

1. Use social media for lead generation

When I run teleseminars and webinars for lead generation, I often ask my email list to share invitations with their Facebook friends. This lets me tap into the Facebook networks of the tens of thousands of people on my mailing list, extending my outreach to probably hundreds of thousands of people. The result is much more attendance and many more leads than I would have gotten on my own. There are many other ways you can generate leads on Facebook and other social media, including posting interesting content on your page like quotes and links to articles and videos, participating in group discussions hosted by other people in your target market, liking others' pages, and sending private messages.

2. Use social media to book appointments

When I was writing this book, I set up an appointment to talk with my book project manager through Facebook. I've found social media works great to book appointments, especially if I just got done hosting an event on social media so the prospect happens to be logged in for the event, making it easy for them to contact me while we're both logged in at the same time. You can also use a social media event to invite someone to contact you for appointment booking through another communication tool like phone or email.

3. Use social media to set the stage for sales

Social media events give you a great vehicle for delivering sales presentations to large groups of people at once. I recently hosted a joint event with several other public speaking experts called Life by Design, where participants were able to join the event on Facebook while the live event was going on. By using this method, we were able to get our front-of-the-room sales pitches in front of our Facebook audience as well as our live audience. It's great leverage when you can take the same time and effort it would normally take you to reach hundreds of live attendees and use it to reach thousands or tens of thousands of people at once!

4. Brand your social media pages

My Facebook pages represent my brand. The graphics and wording of my pages are selected to communicate my personality and the image and message I want to get across to my prospects and customers. One of the things I offer that no other sales trainer offers is the high level of personal support I extend each and every one of my students through weekly phone calls, Facebook discussions, email, and other activities that make me accessible to my students. You can't take Eric Lofholm out of Eric Lofholm International; I'm part of my brand. Put your personality into your product when you design your social media pages.

5. Customize your social media pages

Part of branding your social media pages is customizing them. Most social media tools give you a default design that you can customize with different background graphics, logos, headlines, and navigation features such as menu tabs. For instance, the Life by Design event I mentioned above had a banner introduced by the headline "Eric Lofholm Presents: Life by Design" with a picture of Les Brown on one side and me on the other.

6. Post on a regular schedule

Consistency is the key with social media just as it is with other sales tools. One of the big keys to social media consistency is posting on a regular schedule. If you post every so often and then disappear for a while, people will forget you and your social media outreach won't have any impact. Commit to a regular schedule for your social media postings, whether this is once a day, a few times a week, or once a week.

7. Give others reasons to like and follow you

One of the keys to generating leads on social media is giving others an incentive to pay attention to your social media pages and posts. On Facebook this means giving people a reason to like your page. On Twitter this means giving people a reason to follow you.

Why would people want to like your page or follow you? It might be because you provide interesting content like quotes or pictures. It might be because you link them to interesting content like new articles or videos. It might be because you help publicize their content by liking it or retweeting it. Give people a reason to want to read your social media posts.

8. Give others reasons to click on your links

You also want to give people a reason to click on the links you put in your social media posts. For instance, if you want to get people to watch a new video you just shot, create a short, compelling description of what benefit they would gain from watching the video. Let's say I just shot a video on how to generate more leads by using my POI strategy. I might post the link with an introduction like this: "What's the fastest way to get more leads? Click on this 3-minute video and I'll tell you." Remember to keep your descriptions short when using social media, since tools like Twitter are designed for very short word limits.

9. Use automated social media tools

One of the drawbacks of social media is that it can consume a lot of time. One way around this problem is to use automated social media tools. There are tools that can help you perform tasks like scheduling posts ahead of time, managing lists of followers, and integrating your social media pages with your website and blog content.

10. Use analytics to track your results

If you really want to get the most out of your social media efforts, you should track your results to see what's working and what isn't. Some examples of great tracking tools you can use are Klout, Twitalyzer, and Tweet Reach.

Top 10 Sales Presentation Tips

In earlier parts of this book I gave you step-by-step instructions on how to improve the quality of your sales presentations. Now I'm going to zero in on ten of the biggest keys to successfully executing each step of the process.

1. Have a clear goal for what you want to accomplish during the presentation
2. Script your sales presentations
3. Build rapport with stories
4. Announce your outcomes or agenda
5. Address their pain
6. Sell the benefits
7. Break your content into chunks
8. Structure your close
9. Rehearse answering objections
10. Be prepared to follow up

1. Have a clear goal for what you want to accomplish during the presentation

Prior to delivering your presentation, decide the exact results that you would like to produce. These may be closing the sale, getting five referrals, scheduling the next appointment, or any other step in the sales process. For example, when preparing a webinar, I might set four goals such as to close ten Silver Protégé sales, to be humorous, to have fun, and to make a difference for everyone who listens.

2. Script your sales presentations

I've probably earned more from this tip than any other tip in this book, which is why I'm repeating it here even though you've read it before if you've been following along. Use the scripting techniques from Chapter 13 to script each step in Sales Mountain for your major sales presentations. After you've written your scripts, rehearse them until they come naturally. This is the key to delivering a confident, effective close, time after time for consistent results.

3. Build rapport with stories

Back in Chapter 8 I told you some of the reasons I recommend telling stories during your sales presentations. Among other things, stories can help you build rapport, which makes it a good strategy to include a story towards the beginning of your presentation. You should collect an archive of stories you can use for this purpose, so that you always have stories on hand. As you collect and study stories, you will find it easier to tell stories spontaneously by drawing from your recent experience, experiences of others you know, and recent news.

There are several types of stories you can use to help you build rapport early in your presentation. You might include a story about something you and your prospect have in common that you can use to help establish a common interest, like a story about your spouse or kids or sports or even just the weather. You might tell a story about someone struggling with the same issue your prospect is facing. You might tell a story about someone who used your product or service successfully and the benefits they're experiencing now. You can use stories to anticipate any part of your sales presentation as you build trust and rapport.

4. Announce your outcomes or agenda

Whenever I give a public presentation, I tell my audience at the beginning what I want them to get out of the presentation, including if I'm going to sell them something later. A key to getting the outcome you want from your sales presentation is to announce your outcome early on. This sows the seeds of the outcome in your mind and the mind of your prospect. It also helps you pre-empt objections that might have come up later if you'd waited until the end of your presentation to surprise your prospect with an unexpected sales pitch. Because I told my audience at the beginning that I'd be selling them something later, they won't be as resistant to my sales pitch as they would be if I pretended I was just delivering content and wasn't selling anything and then suddenly surprised them with a sales offer. The fact they knew I was going to sell them something and were still willing to sit through my presentation makes it harder for them to complain later if I offer them something. In fact, it piques their curiosity about what I'm going to sell, making them more likely to buy.

5. Address their pain

Someone in a desert who's dying of thirst will do almost anything to get a drink of water. Someone who's starving will have a hard time concentrating on anything except where they're going to get their next meal. If your prospect has a burning need like this, you can make your offer almost irresistibly compelling by addressing their pain.

Use probing questions to find out what their pain is. Do they need to make more sales to keep their job (like I did)? Do they need to make more money fast to stay in business? Are they stressed out about something? Find what their itch is so you can offer to scratch it.

6. Sell the benefits

You might have heard the saying, "Sell the sizzle, not the steak." This is an example of selling the benefits instead of features, in this case appealing to hunger and taste instead of nutritional value. In Chapter 8 I talked about how to sell benefits. The opposite of this is selling features, which is a mistake almost all sales representatives make.

A good example is the computer industry, where sales representatives often focus so much on technical specifications of hardware and software that they forget to emphasize the practical value to the user. Someone in the market for a PC, laptop, or mobile device doesn't really care how fast the processor is or how much storage space there is. What they care about are things like, can I run my important business software on this without having to buy and install everything I already have all over again? Can I play my favorite video games without crashing in the middle of the game? Can I download my favorite videos from YouTube and Netflix fast enough to enjoy watching them?

Or let's take exercise products as an example. When someone buys a treadmill, do they care how fast the treadmill runs or how fast it makes their heart beat? No. They care about how losing weight will make them feel about themselves. They care about how looking better will make them more attractive to others. They care about how improving their health will make them feel less stress and more energy during the day. Sell the benefits, not the features.

7. Break your content into chunks

It takes time to eat a meal, and it takes time to digest a presentation. Break your presentation up into bite-sized chunks to make it easier to digest. Let your prospect digest each piece of Sales Mountain before you move on to the next one. If you're delivering a long sales presentation in a context like a public speech, use stories, quotes, and visual aids to help break things up into manageable chunks. I usually break my longer public speaking presentations up into three main chunks with stories in between.

8. Structure your close

Closing is easy when you build your close around a solid structure. In Chapter 9 I laid out the typical structure of a successful close: price, what's included, discounts and guarantees, bonuses, incentive to buy now, ask for the order. Following this formula will boost your closing rate and the effectiveness of your overall presentation.

9. Rehearse answering objections

In Chapter 10 I said that there are seven to ten common objections usually encountered by sales representatives in any industry. I then went on to give you fifteen ways to handle any objection. If you want to truly master objection handling as it applies through your industry, go through each of the common objections you're likely to face and use each of the fifteen techniques to come up with as many responses as you can. See if you can come up with ten responses to each objection. Then rehearse your best responses until they become natural.

10. Be prepared to follow up

Many sales aren't closed in one meeting, so making follow-up a vital part of sales success. Even if you do close successfully, you must be prepared to follow up to process the sale.

Make sure you walk into your presentation with a strategy for what you're going to do if the prospect wants to buy now, as well as how you're going to follow up if they don't buy. Make sure you're ready with anything you'll need to take their order, like order forms, phone numbers, or website links. Plan what you're going to do if they say they're not ready to buy today. Are they willing to schedule a follow-up appointment? When will you call them back? What will you say? Will you ask for a referral to someone else? Be prepared to follow up.

Top 10 Closing Tips

Closing is where sales are made or lost. Here are ten of my top secrets to closing success.

1. Embrace a closing mindset
2. A strong opening sets the stage for a strong closing
3. Wait for the sweet spot
4. Script your close
5. Make your offer irresistible
6. Make your offer urgent
7. Ask and be silent
8. Rehearse multiple answers for each objection
9. Get back in the sweet spot if you get out of it
10. Try until they buy or die

1. Embrace a closing mindset

Closing starts with the inner game and your mindset. The same affirmation strategy that applies to selling in general can be adapted to closing to boost your belief in your ability to close. Like selling, closing is a service; closing comes from honesty, integrity, and compassion; closing is about leading and about moving people to action. Closing is a system. A close is the natural conclusion to a well-delivered sales presentation. You can become a master closer by embracing these affirmations.

2. A strong opening sets the stage for a strong closing

Because a close is the natural conclusion to a well-delivered sales presentation, a strong opening sets the stage for a strong closing. If you hone your rapport-building skills, ask good probing questions, and present the benefits your prospect wants, you will already have most of the work of your close done for you. Closing is easy when you set the stage properly.

3. Wait for the sweet spot

In baseball, if you swing too early, you miss. If you swing too late, you miss. If you swing at a ball that's too far off the plate, you miss. Or you might swing at a ball that's too close to the plate and foul it off. A good solid hit comes when you hit the sweet spot, with your bat squarely connecting the right part of the ball at the right angle at the right time.

The same is true of closing. If you close too early, you drive the prospect away. If you wait too long after they're ready to buy, they lose enthusiasm. If you aim your presentation at the wrong prospect, sell a need they're not interested in, or stress the wrong benefit, your sales pitch goes foul. Aim for the sweet spot. Wait for it. Then swing.

4. Script your close

When you script your sales presentations, scripting your close is one of the most important parts. Having a well-scripted, well-rehearsed close gives you the confidence you need to deliver a strong offer and the content you need to make it persuasive. Use the closing structure from Chapter 9 to outline the structure of your closing script: price, what's included, discounts and guarantees, bonuses, incentive to buy now, ask for the order.

5. Make your offer irresistible

When someone is considering whether or not to buy from you, you can picture their decision-making process as being like a teeter-totter. On one side is the reasons you've given them to buy: the benefits. On the other side is the reasons against buying that are weighing on their mind: the risks. Your task is to make the benefits outweigh the risks enough to make them want to buy.

One way to do this is to make your offer irresistible. An irresistible offer is an offer so loaded with benefits and so light on risk that someone would have to be crazy not to take it. You've probably seen commercials for warehouse stores that are running a going out of business sale and offering huge discounts with big bonuses. This is an example of an irresistible offer.

You can make your offer irresistible in two main ways. One is to pack on bonuses and other rewards for buying now. The other is to reduce the risk using techniques like discounts and guarantees. I use both methods at once when I'm designing irresistible offers. For example, in addition to packing on fantastic bonuses to my Unstoppable Selling System program, I often sell the program at a huge discount, and then offer a monthly payment option so low that almost anyone with a credit card should be able to afford it. This makes it very hard for someone to come up with a good reason not to buy my program if they truly want to make more sales.

6. Make your offer urgent

If you were in school and your homework didn't have a due date, would you do it? Probably not. Likewise when you close, you need to add urgency to your close to motivate prospects to take action. There are several time-tested ways you can add urgency, such as limiting the number of available items or spots, limiting the length of a sale, or using other tactics to make an item scarce or exclusive.

7. Ask and be silent

When a Girl Scout asks you if you want to buy a cookie, she waits in silence for your answer. This puts the pressure on you to say "yes" or "no." I call this giving the prospect the hot potato. This is one of the big keys to closing successfully. Learn to ask and be silent. If you have trouble doing this, one trick is to close your fist as a way to manage the tension while you're waiting.

8. Rehearse multiple answers for each objection

Earlier I mentioned that there are seven to ten common objections in any industry. You will close more successfully if you're prepared to meet each of these objections. Script and rehearse multiple answers to each common objection you're likely to face in your industry.

9. Get back in the sweet spot if you get out of it

Sometimes when you follow up, your prospect might have been almost ready to buy earlier, but by the time you get back to them, they've got something else on their mind and they're no longer in the sweet spot. You should always make sure they're back in the sweet spot before trying to close again. Take some time to re-establish trust and rapport and remind them of their previous interest before moving back into the close.

10. Try until they buy or die

A final key to closing is persistence. Many sales take two, three, six, or even twelve or more contacts with the prospect before they decide to buy. A successful closer commits to following up until either the sale is made or the prospect definitely expresses a desire not to buy. I call this tip "try until they buy or die."

Top 10 Goal Setting Ideas

In the first bonus chapter I presented the goal-setting strategy I've used to make my business a success. Here I'll give you ten keys to successfully putting my goal-setting method into practice.

1. Write your goals down
2. Prioritize your goals
3. Make sure you know what your goal will look like when you get there
4. Think of the benefit of the benefit when identifying the motives for pursuing your goals
5. Write down deadlines
6. Write down the path to your goal
7. Create a plan to achieve each step on the path to your goal

8. Schedule action
9. Keep moving forward daily
10. Review your goals daily

1. Write your goals down

Goal-setting works so much more effectively if you write your goals down than if you just pursue your goals in your head. Putting your goals down on paper helps you visualize them, making it easier for your mind to brainstorm and plan. The act of writing your goals down is also a step towards taking action on them. To get the best results with goal-setting, write your goals down.

2. Prioritize your goals

Prioritizing your goals is a key to channeling your energy and resources effectively into pursuing the goals you set. There are several techniques you can use to prioritize your goals. First and foremost, you should identify the goals that are most important for you to achieve and put an emphasis on them. In many cases, these will be long-term goals, so another technique is to identify goals that have more immediate urgency. Finally, you can identify goals that are easy to complete and get out of the way, freeing you up to pursue other goals.

3. Make sure you know what your goal will look like when you get there

This point gets back to what I said in the chapter on goal-setting about making your goals measurable. If you don't know what your goal will look like when you get there, how will you know when you've achieved it? An example of knowing what your goal will look like is setting a weight-loss goal of achieving a specific target weight, say 185 pounds. When you can assign a specific number to a goal, it makes it easier to visualize what you're aiming for. With some intangible goals it's hard to assign a specific number, in which case you can use another way of defining the goal. For instance, if your goal has a series of steps, you can define the goal by defining the steps. You can also use relative terms like "better" or "worse" to define goals in areas like emotional growth or relationship improvement where it might be hard to use numbers. Finally, if you can picture what you'll see or imagine how you'll feel when you achieve your goal, that's another way you can make your goal measurable.

4. Think of the benefit of the benefit when identifying the motives for pursuing your goals

I've told you about the strategy of identifying the benefit of the benefit when you're selling something to someone else. Well, you can use the same strategy to motivate yourself when you're goal-setting! When you get to the step where you're writing down the reasons why you want to pursue your goals, think about the benefit of the benefit. For instance, your goal might be to make more money. But why do you want to make more money? Is it to free yourself from the stress of being in debt? Is it so you can buy your husband or wife that gift you've always wanted to give them but could never afford? Is it so you can give your kids a better future by putting them through college? When you can connect with the benefit of the benefit, your goals will be much more compelling to you.

5. Write down deadlines

Just as you should write down your goals, you should also write down the deadline when you intend to complete your goals. Don't just think it in your head: write it down. This commits your mind and will to action and motivates you to follow through on your commitment.

This technique is even more effective if you write your deadlines down and show them to someone else. In my 90-Day Challenge program, I invite my students to share their goals with our group on Facebook. Publicly committing to a goal like this adds accountability, turning peer pressure to your advantage. There's a power in sharing your goals with others.

6. Write down the path to your goal

Here's another way writing things down can help you achieve your goals. In a notebook, draw a line with an arrow pointing to the right. The left side of the line represents where you are now. The right side where the arrow head is represents where you will be when you achieve your goal. Now break the line into segments by writing down the steps it will take to get you from where you are now to your goal.

This is a simple trick that can be done in a variety of ways to help you visualize the steps to your goal. You could make a list instead of an arrow to accomplish the same thing. Or if you're a good artist or you know how to mindmap, you can also draw the steps to your goal. The point is to visualize the steps you need to take by getting them down on paper.

7. Create a plan to achieve each step on the path to your goal

One trick to turning your goals into results is to map your plan out in specific detail for each step. What will you need to do to complete that step? What physical resources will you need, such as space or equipment? What skills will you need? Can you do it yourself or will you need to hire anyone? How much money will it cost? How much time will it take? Ideally you should know exactly what you need to do for each step and have a rough estimate of how much time it will take.

8. Schedule action

What doesn't get scheduled, doesn't get done. You will get the best results from your goal-setting if you schedule blocks of time to take the actions needed to make your goals a reality. This is why I've included tips on time management in this book.

9. Keep moving forward daily

Commit to moving forward towards your goals daily, even if it's a small step at a time. If you keep taking enough steps forward, you will eventually walk a thousand miles. But you can't get anywhere by moving still. Some days you'll get a lot done, and some days you'll only get a little done, but keep getting something done and you will get there.

10. Review your goals daily

Part of your goal-setting strategy should include building a daily review of your goals into your routine. I recommend 14 minutes a day every morning for my students, and I require it of my employees. Use this daily time to view your goals on paper, visualize them in your mind, and say them aloud.

Top 10 Time Management Ideas

In the second bonus chapter I told you the time management strategy I use to turn my goals into reality. Here I'm going to give you ten keys to putting my time management system into action.

1. Budget your time like you budget money
2. Prioritize leveraged activities that produce results
3. Ask questions to plan your optimum day
4. Include both sales and non-sales items
5. Spend 14 minutes a day planning
6. Plan your day in writing
7. List and prioritize
8. Combine activities that can be combined
9. Eliminate activities that can be eliminated
10. Don't beat yourself up when you don't follow through

1. Budget your time like you budget money

You can budget your time like you budget money. There are 168 hours a week. Most people spend about 56 of these on sleep, leaving about 112 left. Of these most people spend another 20 to 40 on work, and another 8 to 10 on activities like church and recreation. What do you spend your waking time on? What can you do in 112 hours? Where can you save time to give yourself time for more important things?

2. Prioritize leveraged activities that produce results

When deciding how to spend your time, the wise strategy is to leverage your time by prioritizing the activities that produce the results you want. A business management rule of thumb called the Pareto principle is that most businesses get 80 percent of their results from 20 percent of their activities. Are you devoting that key 20 percent of your time to the most productive activities you could be pursuing? Or are you prioritizing activities that aren't producing results?

3. Ask questions to plan your optimum day

A technique to help you get the results you want from the time you spend is to plan your optimum, ideal day. If you could imagine your ideal day, what would it look like? What time would you get up? How would you feel when you got up? What would you do with your morning? How would you spend your afternoon and evening? What would you do before bed? When would you go to bed? Asking these kinds of questions to help you visualize your ideal day and write it down on paper can help you in structuring your time to get the results you want.

4. Include both sales and non-sales items

This is a book about sales, but to be effective at sales, you need a lifestyle that supports your pursuit of your sales goals. This is why I've included tips on other areas of your life like goal-setting, time management, health, and relationships. Spirituality is another big area of life not covered in this book. When devising your time management strategy, make sure you remember to include non-sales activities as part of the big picture.

5. Spend 14 minutes a day planning

When giving goal-setting tips, I recommended that you spend 14 minutes a day reviewing your goals. Make sure you include this time block for reviewing your goals when you're planning your weekly time budget.

6. Plan your day in writing

Just as writing your goals down is key to getting goal-setting results, planning your day in writing is key to getting time management results. Use a calendar, a notebook, or another tool to write down your schedule. If your schedule is complicated, you should consider using automated calendar tools like Outlook. This especially applies to sales representatives who have many appointments a day to manage.

7. List and prioritize

Just as you can prioritize your goals, you can also prioritize the tasks on your schedule. When planning your schedule, list the tasks you need to accomplish and then prioritize them. Which tasks are most important to get done to achieve your long-term goals? Which are most urgent to get done first? Which can be accomplished quickly to get them out of the way?

8. Combine activities that can be combined

Look for ways to save time by combining activities you can do at once. A simple example is when you can run several errands on one trip instead of making a number of separate trips. Take this simple strategy and see how you can apply it in your business and sales activity. For instance, instead of making a number of contacts with individual prospects, you might find you can save time by delivering a group presentation to many prospects at once.

9. Eliminate activities that can be eliminated

Another way to save time is by eliminating unnecessary activities. Most people do any number of things that could be cut out of their routine. A good example is answering emails individually, which can take hours out of your day. You can cut down on the time you spend answering emails by developing an email management system where you use automated tools to sort your email by priority and then set aside a specific block of time to answer priority emails.

10. Don't beat yourself up when you don't follow through

Some days you won't get everything done that you had planned. It may be that you underestimated the time required. It may be that something urgent came up. It may be you got sick. Whatever the reason, it happens. When this happens, don't waste time beating yourself up. Commit to continuing to move forward tomorrow by picking up where you left off.

Top 10 Health Tips

You might be wondering what health has to do with sales and why I'm including health tips in this book. There are several reasons. One is that in order to have the energy you need to take action on sales, you need to stay healthy. Two is that you can apply the same strategies to health that you can to sales by borrowing the distinctions of inner game, outer game, and action. Finally, you can learn a lot about selling by studying how health clubs market themselves. Some of my sales training programs are actually modeled on an exercise program I participate in to stay in shape. I train under a fitness coach who also trains MMA fighters and puts me through some pretty intense workouts. Here are ten ways to give you the health habits you need to sustain your energy for sales.

1. Develop a healthy mindset
2. Set an intention to pursue good health
3. Create a health strategy
4. Drink more water
5. Eat smarter, not less
6. Substitute healthy snacks for junk food
7. Exercise in moderate chunks
8. Set health goals
9. Schedule health activities
10. Make health a habit

1. Develop a healthy mindset

One of the biggest reasons sales people and other business people don't pursue good health habits is because they have a mindset that "I'm too busy to take time to pay attention for my health" or "I don't have time for exercise" or similar notions. When you have this attitude, you have no motivation to take care of your health. If this characterizes you, you should tell yourself how important your health is to your business success. Your health affects your energy level, which affects your work output. Better health means more energy, more energy means more sales. Your personal health impacts your financial health. Not to mention getting sick can be expensive!

2. Set an intention to pursue good health

Another part of developing a healthy mindset is setting an intention to pursue good health. When you commit yourself to living a more healthy lifestyle, your actions begin to follow your intention. I recently committed to a 90-day exercise challenge. The benefits I got from declaring this intention spilled over into other areas of my life, pushing my business to new levels as I pushed my body to the goal I had committed to.

3. Create a health strategy

Just as you need a sales strategy, you also need a health strategy. A complete health strategy includes diet and exercise, as well as things like breathing, sleep, posture, ergonomics, and medical and dental check-ups. You can also look at strategy in terms of the different parts of the body and the different systems that make up the body: skeleton, muscles, the cardiovascular system, the digestive system, and so on.

4. Drink more water

Your body is mostly water, making sufficient water intake a key to good health. Exactly how much water you should drink depends on your body type and size and physical activity level. If you do sports or work in a hot environment, one thing to remember is that you start to get dehydrated before you feel thirsty, so you should keep up your fluid intake regardless of your thirst level.

5. Eat smarter, not less

Dietary strategy is a major part of any health strategy. Some people try to lose weight by starving themselves and eating food they don't like, which almost never works. Even if you lose weight that way, chances are you'll soon gain it back. A more effective dietary strategy is to eat smarter, not less. For instance, eating a number of small, healthy meals throughout the day will help keep you from getting hungry enough to overeat at any one meal.

6. Substitute healthy foods for junk foods

One way to eat smarter is to substitute healthy foods for junk foods. For instance, instead of potato chips, you might substitute another type of snack cracker with less fat. This strategy lets you eat enough so you don't get hungry, while still avoiding unhealthy foods that cause you to gain weight.

7. Exercise in moderate chunks

I follow a pretty strenuous exercise program because I like to push myself, but for most people, exercising in moderate chunks is a more reasonable goal. It's better to exercise a little bit regularly than to set off on an ambitious exercise program only to quit a few days later because you overdid it and now you don't feel motivated.

8. Set health goals

The concept of GSA also applies to your health. Set health goals the same way you set sales goals. My 90-day exercise challenge includes specific goals I plan to achieve during that time period.

9. Schedule health activities

You can schedule health activities the same way you schedule sales activities. Setting a regular exercise schedule is a big part of this. You should also schedule other important activities like getting regular sleep and going in for regular medical and dental check-ups.

10. Make health a habit

Health results don't happen overnight, but they come from regular, consistent actions that become habits. Take actions like changing your diet and exercise patterns on a consistent schedule from day to day, week to week, month to month, year to year, and you will see growth over time.

Top 10 Relationship Tips

Like health, relationships have more to do with sales than it might seem at first. When you think about it, selling is a relationship between the sales representative and the prospect. You can't have rapport without having a relationship with your prospect. But you don't learn rapport first in a sales context. You learn it in other relationships, with your parents, with your children, in your home, at school, at church. Here are ten tips for building stronger relationships to lay a solid foundation for your sales relationships.

1. Cultivate a compassionate mindset
2. Commit to successful relationships
3. Set the example by focusing on changing yourself first
4. Appreciate other people's gifts
5. Build rapport by listening
6. Use probing questions to learn what others like and dislike
7. Use constructive criticism delicately

8. Avoid arguing when angry

9. Use relationship scripts

10. Set aside special times for building relationships

1. Cultivate a compassionate mindset

The Golden Rule for relationships is, "Do unto others as you would have them to unto you." This requires getting out of yourself enough to appreciate how another person feels and sees things, which involves compassion. Develop a compassionate mindset by repeating affirmations that make you more aware of others' perspectives and feelings.

2. Commit to successful relationships

Why do so many marriages end in divorce? There are many reasons, but one common reason is mindset. Many people enter marriage with the idea that divorce is an option. That option has never been part of my thinking. My mindset is that I still want to be married when I'm 70 years old. Because I have that mindset, I'm committed to doing what it takes to make my marriage work. As a result, although my marriage has had its ups and downs, my wife and I have stayed together, through better and through worse. Commit to success in your relationships.

3. Set the example by focusing on changing yourself first

In my experience as a husband, I don't have much luck getting my wife to do things by nagging her about things I don't like. That might get me sleeping on the couch, but it's not going to get me positive results! I get much better results when I take the initiative to change myself first. I ask myself what I can do to improve my relationship with my wife and our children. I often find that when I make the first effort, my wife and kids reciprocate.

4. Appreciate other people's gifts

To divert yourself from trying to change other people, you can focus instead on appreciating their gifts. Start noticing what people are good at and complimenting them on it. You will find this makes you feel more positive towards them, and it will make them feel more positive towards you.

5. Build rapport by listening

Rapport isn't just for sales. You can also use rapport in your relationships. One of the most basic ways to build rapport is by becoming a better listener. As the saying goes, God gave us one mouth but two ears. Listening more is a big step towards enhancing the rapport in your relationships.

6. Use probing questions to learn what others like and dislike

Probing questions can help you make sales, and they can also help you improve your relationships. Ask questions to find out what people around you like and dislike. This will help you be more attuned to the needs of people around you.

7. Use constructive criticism delicately

In sales we handle objections; in relationships we handle criticisms, which often lead to arguments. How you handle giving criticism is one of the big factors that influences the quality of your relationships. Criticisms should normally be delivered privately, delicately, and infrequently. The opposite of this is nagging, which is one of the biggest destroyers of relationships. Handle criticisms delicately.

8. Avoid arguing when angry

Another aspect of objection handling in relationships is how you handle arguments. Arguing when you're angry is an almost sure way to escalate a disagreement into a fight, and the more you do it the more it chips away at your relationships. You'll have a much more productive conversations and a better relationship if you take a step back and wait to cool down before continuing the discussion in a calmer mood.

9. Use relationship scripts

If I kept telling my kids, "Why don't you ever clean your room?", I'd be subconsciously programming them not to clean their room, and it wouldn't be a surprise if they never cleaned their room. Instead, we play a game called "BSE12". This stands for "Brandon, Sarah, and Eric clean for 12 minutes while Mom takes a break." I can call BSE12 at any time, and my son Brandon and my daughter Sarah will join me in cleaning the house. This is a script we use to make cleaning a habit in our home. You can use scripts like this in any relationship, in your family life, in dating relationships, or in relationships at work.

10. Set aside special times for building relationships

You can apply time management strategies to relationships just as you can to sales. One strategy that helps improve the quality of your relationships is to set aside special times for building them. For instance, setting aside time for church every Sunday is a way to build your relationship with God. Every weekend and throughout the week I also set aside time for my family. In a business context, many companies have picnics and other team-building recreational events. Invest time in building your relationships.

Top 10 Success Habits

I'm going to close out this bonus section of the book by giving you ten secrets that have been keys to my success. I've learned about success by studying under people like Tony Robbins, who has spent decades studying the habits of successful people. Some of these tips come from Tony, others come from my other mentors, and all come from my own experience applying these strategies to become a successful sales trainer. Here are ten tips to help you achieve success at achieving your sales goals and goals in other areas of your life.

1. Model successful people
2. Model your own successes
3. Cultivate a successful mindset
4. Practice successful goal-setting habits
5. Set high goals
6. Practice successful time management habits
7. Use small victories to build bigger ones
8. Learn from your mistakes
9. Apply success strategies to all areas of your life
10. Persevere

1. Model successful people

One of the biggest keys to my success has been modeling successful people. I modeled master sales trainer Donald Moine to learn sales. I modeled master public speaker Tony Robbins to learn public speaking. I modeled master marketing consultant Jay Abraham to learn marketing. Right now I'm modeling an

MMA trainer to improve my health. The shortest way to become successful is to copy successful people.

2. Model your own successes

You can also model your own successes! We each have our gifts and our moments. There are some things you are better at than others. There are some things you can do better than anyone else. There have been times in your life when you performed at your peak, when you were on your game, when you aced it. Take an inventory of these successes, and notice what you did differently at those times than other times in your life. Notice what you're good at, and what you do differently when you do those things compared to what you do elsewhere in your life. Study your own success formula, and apply it to areas of your life where you'd like to be more successful.

3. Cultivate a successful mindset

The foundation of success is a successful inner game, centered around a successful mindset. Build a successful mindset by repeating affirmations like those you used to cultivate your sales mindset, applied to other areas of your life where you'd like to be successful. Here are some examples: "I'm going to play at a 7 or higher today." "I'm going to get in the best shape of my life over the next 90 days." "I'm going to make my wife feel special for her birthday this month." "I'm going to add $1,000 a week to my income this quarter." Design your own affirmations focused on your own success goals, and repeat them to yourself daily.

4. Practice successful goal-setting habits

Almost all success coaches recommend goal-setting as a key strategy. I've studied many goal-setting systems and given you my best golden nuggets in this book. Make goal-setting a cornerstone of your success strategy by making it a regular part of your routine.

5. Set high goals

During my 90-Day Challenge, I invite my students to set outrageous goals, goals that seem higher than they could achieve. Why do I do this? Because setting a high goal raises your mental bar. It forces you to try harder, which makes it more likely you will achieve your goal. Even if you fall short of your goal, the fact you set a high goal means that you will still achieve respectable results even if they're not quite the results you aimed for. But if you set a low goal and fail, you just fail. Set your goals high to push yourself to success.

6. Practice successful time management habits

Goals without action are just dreams. The bridge between goals and action is time management. If you want to make your goals a reality, apply the time management strategies I've presented in these bonus chapters and schedule time to make your goals happen.

7. Use small victories to build bigger ones

Sometimes it just takes a spark to set a forest on fire. Sometimes a small dam is all that's holding back a flood. Sometimes all it takes is one small victory to start the snowball of success rolling. The first month I started applying Dr. Moine's sales system, I made my quota by just one sale. It was a small victory, but it was enough to create the opportunity I needed. One month later I was the top sales representative in my department. I had had a breakthrough. Your next small victory could be the breakthrough you've been waiting for.

8. Learn from your mistakes

Describing his struggle to improve the light bulb, Thomas Edison said, "I haven't failed. I've just found 10,000 ways that won't work." We all make mistakes. It took a lot of mistakes to get me to the point where I almost lost my first sales job. I've made more mistakes since starting my own business. But I learned from my mistakes. I found out what I was doing wrong and I took the steps I needed to improve. I wouldn't have gained that knowledge if I hadn't made the mistake in the first place so I knew there was a problem that needed to be solved. Some people are afraid to start because they're afraid of making a mistake. But the only way you don't make mistakes is if you don't try, which is a sure way not to succeed at anything. Don't be afraid to make mistakes: commit to learning from them instead.

9. Apply success strategies to all areas of your life

When you find a successful strategy that works in one area of your life, you can copy it in other areas of your life. This is a book about sales success, but as I've tried to show you in these closing pages, the success strategies I've applied to sales can also help you in other areas of your life. Take the success strategies you've learned in this book to help your sales, and use them to help you grow in your health, your relationships, your spirituality, and other important areas of your life as well as your finances. Commit to being successful in all areas of your life, and sales success will follow.

10. Persevere

One of my favorite metaphors for sales success is the story of the Tortoise and the Hare. The hare is faster, but also lazier, so he starts off strong, but then he lays down and rests on his laurels. The tortoise is slower, but more determined, so he's able to finish and win while the hare is sleeping on the job. Sales is a marathon, not a sprint. Persevere to the end, and you will win. And congratulations on persevering to the end of this book!

My Success Journal Notes

Use the following blank pages to declare your success intention and record the best ideas you learn from each chapter. As you learn and take action, identify the ten best ideas you're learning and, applying the 80/20 rule, focus on applying those ideas one at a time to improving your sales results and business performance.

Success Intention:

I, _____ declare my intention to succeed at sales by studying this book and applying its ideas.

_____ Date

(After filling in your intention, let me know by sending me an email with the subject line "Success intention" at **wins@ericlofholm.com**!)

Notes:
Introduction

Notes:
Part I: The Inner Game of Selling

Notes:
Chapter 1: Mindset

_____

_____

_____

_____

_____

_____

_____

_____

_____

_____

_____

_____

_____

_____

_____

_____

_____

_____

_____

_____

_____

_____

_____

_____

_____

_____

_____

Notes:
Chapter 2: What I Learned from
One of the World's Greatest Thinkers

Notes:
Part II: The Outer Game of Selling

Notes:
Chapter 3: The Process of Influence

Notes:
Chapter 4: Generating Unlimited Leads

Notes:
Chapter 5: Setting Unlimited Appointments

Notes:
Chapter 6: Building Instant Trust and Rapport

Notes:
Chapter 7: Identifying Needs

Notes:
Chapter 8: The Real Reason People Buy

_____

_____

_____

_____

_____

_____

_____

_____

_____

_____

_____

_____

_____

_____

_____

_____

_____

_____

_____

_____

_____

_____

_____

_____

_____

_____

Notes:
Chapter 9: Closing

Notes:
Chapter 10: The Elegant Dance—Objections

Notes:
Chapter 11: The Fortune in the Follow-up

Notes:
Chapter 12: Generating Unlimited Referrals

Notes:
Chapter 13: Sales Scripting

Notes:
Chapter 14: GSA (Goals, Strategy, Action)

_____

_____

_____

_____

_____

_____

_____

_____

_____

_____

_____

_____

_____

_____

_____

_____

_____

_____

_____

_____

_____

_____

_____

_____

_____

_____

Notes:
Part III: Action

Notes:
Chapter 15: Putting It All Together

Notes:
Bonus Chapter #1: Goal Setting Mastery

Notes:
Bonus Chapter 2: Time Management Success System

_____

_____

_____

_____

_____

_____

_____

_____

_____

_____

_____

_____

_____

_____

_____

_____

_____

_____

_____

_____

_____

_____

_____

_____

_____

_____

_____

_____

Notes:
Bonus Chapter 3: Lofholmisms

Notes:
Bonus Chapter 4: Top 150 Secrets of Success

_____

_____

_____

_____

_____

_____

_____

_____

_____

_____

_____

_____

_____

_____

_____

_____

_____

_____

_____

_____

_____

_____

_____

_____

_____

_____

_____

Notes:
The 10 Best Ideas I'm Learning from This Book

(Extra lines included so you can add as you learn.)

_____

_____

_____

_____

_____

_____

_____

_____

_____

_____

_____

_____

_____

_____

_____

_____

_____

_____

_____

_____

_____

_____

_____

_____

_____

_____

_____

_____

Glossary

Affirmation: A key word or phrase repeated to reinforce mindset.

Appointment booking: The act of scheduling a sales presentation meeting with a prospect. Distinct from lead generation and from delivering sales presentations.

Ask and be silent: A closing technique where you extend an offer and then remain silent while waiting for the prospect's response. Related to "hot potato."

Baseline: Your current sales performance numbers in areas such as leads, appointments, and sales generated over a specific time frame. Related to "track to run on."

Benefit of the benefit: An unstated or ulterior appeal associated with a stated benefit. (See "benefits.")

Benefits: Practical values of products or services. Distinct from "features."

Closing: The part of a sales presentation where you make the prospect a sales offer by offering them value in exchange for a price.

Database: A manual or automated system for managing contact information of prospects and clients.

Features: Descriptions of the components or specifications of products or services. Distinct from "benefits."

Follow-up: The part of the sales process where you resume contact with a prospect following the initial sales presentation.

Goal setting: A step-by-step procedure for systematically naming, prioritizing, and pursuing goals.

GSA (Goal Strategy Action): The three steps in putting a sales system into practical operation.

Hot potato: A closing or probing question technique where you put the burden of responding to a question or offer on the prospect until they reply, whereupon their reply returns the "hot potato" to you. Related to "ask and be silent."

Lead: A prospective customer.

Lead generation: The act of adding leads to your database by finding prospective customers, reaching them, and collecting their contact information.

Mindset: The habitual beliefs and attitudes that underlie your sales performance.

Objection handling: The part of a sales presentation after the close where you respond to prospect concerns about making a purchase.

Pre-client funnel: A technique for optimizing lead generation where you seek to funnel qualified prospects towards you while discouraging unqualified prospects.

Precession: The principle that action creates results and momentum that can have unexpected benefits, which would not occur if action were not being taken.

Prospect: A potential customer.

Prospecting: The part of the sales process where you seek to add leads to your database and establish contact with them.

Rapport: The act of establishing and nurturing a positive relationship of trust with your prospect. Underlies all other steps in the sales process.

Sales scripting: Writing and rehearsing sales presentations for optimal sequencing, wording, and delivery.

Sales Mountain: The step-by-step process for generating leads, booking appointments, and delivering sales presentations taught by Eric Lofholm.

Time management: A step-by-step procedure for systematically scheduling activities to meet priorities while saving time and energy.

Touches: The number of pre-sales contacts you make with leads in your database.

Track to run on: The number of leads, appointments, and sales you need to make to reach your sales targets. Related to "baseline."

Upsell: A sales strategy for selling related products and services to customers who have already bought from you.

80/20 rule (Pareto principle): A time management principle which advises spending 80 percent of your time on the 20 percent of activities responsible for generating the bulk of your business results.

For Further Reading

Abraham, Jay. *Getting Everything You Can Out of All You've Got: 21 Ways You Can Out-Think, Out-Perform, and Out-Earn the Competition.* New York: St. Martin's Press, 2000.

Aspley, John Cameron. *Aspley on Sales: A Guide to Selling in the Modern Market.* Chicago: Dartnell Corporation, 1967.

Belch, George E. and Michael A. *Advertising and Promotion: An Integrated Marketing Communications Perspective.* New York: McGraw-Hill/Irwin, 2011.

Bettger, Frank. *How I Multiplied My Income and Happiness in Selling.* New York: Prentice Hall Press, 1982.

Bettger, Frank. *How I Raised Myself from Failure to Success in Selling.* New York: Prentice Hall Press, 1986 (1947).

Burg, Bob. *Endless Referrals.* Third edition. New York: McGraw-Hill, 2005 (1994).

Butler, Ralph Starr, Herbert F. De Bower, and John G. Jones. *Marketing Methods and Salesmanship.* New York: Alexander Hamilton Institute, 1914.

Carnegie, Dale. *How to Win Friends & Influence People.* New York: Simon & Schuster, 1981 (1936).

Cialdini, Robert B., Ph.D. *Influence: The Psychology of Persuasion.* New York: Collins, 2007.

Feldman, Ben. *Creative Selling: The World's Greatest Life Insurance Salesman Answers Your Questions.* New York: Farnsworth Publishing Company, 1974.

Fenton, Richard and Andrea Waltz. *Go for No! Yes is the Destination, No is How You Get There.* Orlando: Courage Crafters, 2010.

Gamble, Teri and Michael. *Sales Scripts That Sell!* New York: AMACOM, 1992.

Gay III, Ben F. *The Closers*. Placerville: Hampton Books, 1987.

Gay III, Ben F. *The Closers: Part II*. Placerville: Hampton Books, 2000.

Getty, J. Paul. *How to Be Rich*. Chicago: Playboy Press, 1965.

Girard, Joe. With Stanley H. Brown. *How to Sell Anything to Anybody*. New York: Warner Books, 1977.

Gittomer, Jeffrey. *The Sales Bible: The Ultimate Sales Resource*. New edition. New York: HarperBusiness, 2008 (New York: William Morrow, 1994).

Good, Bill. *Prospecting Your Way to Sales Success: How to Find New Business by Phone, Fax, Internet and Other New Media*. New York: Scribner, 1997 (1986).

Hall, Roland S. *The Handbook of Sales Management: A Review of Modern Sales Practice and Management*. New York: McGraw-Hill, 1924.

Hickerson, J.M. *How I Made the Sale That Did the Most for Me: Sixty Great Sales Stories Told by Sixty Great Salesmen*. New York: Prentice Hall, 1951.

Hogan, Kevin. *The Psychology of Persuasion: How to Persuade Others to Your Way of Thinking*. Gretna: Pelican Publishing Company, 1996.

Holmes, Chet. *The Ultimate Sales Machine: Turbocharge Your Business with Relentless Focus on 12 Key Strategies*. New York: Penguin Group, 2007.

Hopkins, Tom. *How to Master the Art of Selling*. Introduction by J. Douglas Edwards. Fully updated and revised. New York: Business Plus, 2005 (first edition 1980).

Hoyt, Charles Wilson. *Scientific Sales Management: A Practical Application of the Principles of Scientific Management to Selling*. New Haven: George B. Woolson & Company, 1913.

Klaff, Oren. *Pitch Anything: An Innovative Method for Presenting, Persuading, and Winning the Deal*. New York: McGraw-Hill, 2011.

Kroc, Ray. With Robert Anderson. *Grinding It Out: The Making of McDonald's*. Chicago: Contemporary Books, 1977.

Kuesel, Harry K. *Kuesel on Closing Sales*. New York: Prentice Hall, 1979.

Kuesel, Harry N. *How to Sell Against Tough Competition*. New York: Prentice Hall, 1958.

Miller, Robert B. and Stephen E. Heiman. With Tad Tuleja. *The New Strategic Selling: The Unique Sales System Proven Successful by America's Best Companies*. Revised and updated with a new preface by Robert B. Miller. New York: Business Plus, 2005 (1998; first edition New York: Warner Books, 1985).

Moine, Donald, Ph.D. and Kenneth Lloyd, Ph.D. *Ultimate Selling Power: How to Create and Enjoy a Multimillion Dollar Sales Career*. Franklin Lakes: Career Press, 2002.

Moine, Donald, Ph.D. and Kenneth Lloyd, Ph.D. *Unlimited Selling Power: How to Master Hypnotic Selling Skills*. Englewood Cliffs: Prentice Hall, 1990.

Parinello, Anthony. *Selling to VITO: The Very Important Top Officer*. Third edition. Avon: Adams Media Corporation, 2010 (1994).

Person, H.S. (editor). *Scientific Management in American Industry*. New York: Harper & Brothers, 1929.

Pickens, James W. *The One Minute Closer: Time-Tested, No-Fail Strategies for Clinching Every Sale*. New York: Business Plus, 2008.

Popeil, Ron. With Jefferson Graham. *The Salesman of the Century: Inventing Marketing, and Selling on TV: How I Did It and How You Can Too!* New York: Delacorte Press, 1995.

Port, Michael. *Book Yourself Solid: The Fastest, Easiest, and Most Reliable System for Getting More Clients Than You Can Handle Even if You Hate Marketing and Selling*. Foreword by Tim Sanders. Hoboken: Wiley, 2006.

Rackham, Neil. *SPIN Selling*. Aldershot, England: Gower, 1995 (first published in 1987 as *Making Major Sales*).

Rackham, Neil. *The SPIN Selling Fieldbook: Practical Tools, Methods, Exercises, and Resources*. New York: McGraw-Hill, 1996.

Robbins, Anthony. *Awaken the Giant Within*. New York: Simon & Schuster, 1992.

Robbins, Anthony. *Unlimited Power: The New Science of Personal Achievement*. New York: Simon & Schuster, 1986.

Rosenstein, J.L. *The Scientific Selection of Salesmen*. New York: McGraw-Hill, 1944.

Sandler, David H. With John Hayes, Ph.D. *You Can't Teach a Kid to Ride a Bike at a Seminar: The Sandler Sales Institute's 7-Step System for Successful Selling*. New York: Dutton, 1995.

Schiffman, Stephan. *Power Sales Presentations: Complete Sales Dialogues for Each Critical Step of the Sale Cycle*. Holbrook, Massachussetts: Adams Media Corporation, 1993 (1989).

Scott, Walter Dill. *Aids in Selecting Salesmen*. Pittsburgh: Bureau of Salesmanship Research, Carnegie Institute of Technology, 1916.

Strong, Edward K. *The Psychology of Selling and Advertising*. New York: McGraw-Hill, 1925.

Strong, Edward K. *The Psychology of Selling Life Insurance*. New York: Harper & Brothers, 1922.

Thomson, Andrew H. With Lee Rosler. *The Feldman Method: The Words and Philosophy of the World's Greatest Insurance Salesman*. New York: Farnsworth Publishing Company, 1980.

Thompson, Willard Mead. *The Basics of Successful Salesmanship: A Self-Teaching Programmed Book*. New York: McGraw-Hill, 1968.

Tracy, Brian. *Advanced Selling Strategies: The Proven System of Sales Ideas, Methods, and Techniques Used by Top Salespeople Everywhere*. New York: Fireside, 1995.

Tracy, Brian. *The Psychology of Selling: How to Sell More, Easier and Faster than You Ever Thought Possible*. Nashville: Thomas Nelson, 2004.

Ziglar, Zig. *Zig Ziglar's Secrets of Closing the Sale*. Grand Rapids: Fleming H. Revell Company, 1984.

Ziglar, Zig. *Ziglar on Selling: The Ultimate Handbook for the Complete Sales Professional*. Nashville: Thomas Nelson, 2003 (1991).

Index

About Eric Lofholm

ERIC LOFHOLM has helped over 10,000 students improve their sales results. Eric was not a natural born salesman, but was forced to learn sales fast when he found his first sales job on the line in 1993. Desperate after receiving a one-month probation warning from his supervisor, Eric turned to bestselling sales trainer Dr. Donald Moine for help. Using Dr. Moine's system, Eric managed to make his monthly quota by just one sale and keep his job. By the end of the next month, he had quintupled his sales and become the top producer on his team. Soon everyone wanted to know the secret of his success. Eric began sharing his sales secrets with his coworkers, and soon discovered he had a natural gift for teaching.

Eric honed his sales training skills as a trainer for Tony Robbins for three years from 1997 to 1999. He then founded his own sales training company, Eric Lofholm International. He offers affordable training both for corporate sales departments and for individual entrepreneurs who want to improve their sales skills.

Eric lives in Rocklin, California with his children Brandon and Sarah.

To Learn More

If you liked what you learned in this book and you'd like to learn more, your next step is to sign up for my virtual sales training opportunities. My four-level sales training system is designed to give you a "Black Belt in Influence," providing you with everything you need to progress from basic sales skills to becoming a master sales person yourself.

I offer live training events, but for your convenience, I also provide online sales training opportunities. You can learn directly from me from the comfort of your own computer or mobile device!

You can register yourself for *free* by visiting this link:

http://www.saleschampion.com